ACTIVE INVESTING FOR FINANCIAL FREEDOM – AN INTRODUCTION TO SPECIAL SITUATIONS IN THE STOCK MARKET

- **AN ALTERNATIVE WAY TO ACHIEVE F.I.R.E. AS PASSIVE INDEX INVESTING IN EQUITIES IS UNDER THREAT**

CHAPTER 1 - About the author and why have I written this book?

My name is Steve Green and you may have come across this book from previously reading my blog at
https://valueinvestingforaliving.com/

Or you may have typed the wrong thing into google.

There are three main reasons that quickly spring to mind why I wrote this book. I shall elaborate below.

1) Very few in the FIRE community invest outside of passive index ETFs

By the way I haven't even really thought of myself as having achieved "FIRE" (Financial Independence Retire Early). There are parts of it that I don't relate to that well. I am probably frugal when it comes to big ticket items or expenditures. For example think of cars, accommodation, furnishings, acquiring other recreational "things" etc. On the other hand I am the opposite to many in the FIRE community who try to cut back in other areas. For instance travel, coffee and alcohol have been areas I arguably splurge in. Those areas have very much had a detrimental effect on my wealth, but I am perfectly happy that has been the case.

I also haven't really thought about retirement, at least the way some describe it anyway. Personally, I assume I will always have a passion for investing in the share market. This may take up at least more than half of the hours of a traditional working week. I can't foresee that ever changing. So in that sense I am likely to be "working" (as I expect this to produce financial rewards) until the day I drop!

I did however quit a normal full time role in the investment industry when I was 42 years old. I am not that optimistic though that good easy future investment returns are there to be had. Therefore I haven't ever had the thought that I could sit on the couch, do and earn nothing for the rest of my life. Having said that, I am perfectly at ease in potentially spending a year or two pursuing something that interests me that may pay me nothing. In my first year from the workforce that led me to some charity work and study, amongst other things. So perhaps that ticks off the "FI" part in FIRE for me? I hear that writing an eBook in 2020 is likely to earn you bugger all also, so that is another example!

So what were the main reasons I was able to leave the workforce when I did? Unlike most in the FIRE community I read about, pursuing an extreme savings strategy and using passive index ETFs played no role. I was fortunate to earn better than most in terms of my salary whilst working in the investment industry, so I cannot underestimate the significance of that. I am sure most realise though that a high salary alone is not good enough to achieve financial freedom. Most of us probably know someone in their wider circle of friends or work colleagues who struggle to save anything on extremely high earnings. Or invest the money poorly.

For me a key reason in quitting the workforce earlier than most was solid investment returns above that of the major equity benchmarks. To do this you obviously need a portfolio quite different to the benchmarks. You also need the faith in your strategies to continue implementing them even during the tough times. There are likely to be long periods of when a simple passive index ETF would have performed better.

To be honest I also got lucky in my opinion using some margin loan leverage from around 2002 to 2006. I again was using leverage, but via a line of credit on my main residence, from late 2008 until 2015. In hindsight I think that latter use of leverage made more sense compared with the way I handled things pre GFC. My main point is for me personally, if I just restricted my mindset to index ETFs I might well still be in the workforce in 2020. Or more likely be quitting my job at this stage or possibly in the last year or two. I am guessing I would have stayed in the workforce almost 5 years later than I actually did do though. So investment returns helped me considerably. I will touch on such returns in a more detailed manner in a later chapter.

Unfortunately I will limit the investment returns discussion to the 5 year period after I quit my job though. This is when my self-managed retirement fund has been running and has been audited.

My book will detail about how I went about investing since the mid-1990s and continue to do so. It may or may not contain strategies that are useful for you. I can't decide on that. This is just my experience. As very few in the FIRE community seem to consider venturing outside of ETFs, I thought my experience might be interesting for some.

Having said that though, I concede that the majority of readers should not try these methods. They require a high level of enthusiasm for picking your own direct stocks in the market. This intern requires a significant number of hours each week of time. Also it requires a high degree of confidence to stick to your methods when they have a bad run.

2) I want to write something a young person would understand

I still don't consider writing to be a strength of mine, it may even be a weakness! I began a blog in early 2016 after pretty much zero writing experience since my high school / university days. Setting goals to improve in certain areas can be quite fulfilling. This book is a challenging goal of mine I set in 2020.

I surprised myself that I continued blogging for another four years after I began in 2016. A lot of my investment strategies in this book have been touched on in the blog. The shorter format of blogging though can have its difficulties in conveying a message. I have felt that it is difficult to write in a style where a less experienced investor can see the merits in my strategies. My son was only recently born in 2019. Sometimes I have wondered if he could learn much from reading my blog when he gets into is 20s.

Therefore that is in the back of my mind when writing this book. I want to assume a reader has already have had perhaps a couple of years investing in the stock market. Maybe owned some ETFs, picked an individual stock or two themselves. They may have tried reading some balance sheets and company presentations but not devoted a huge amount of time to it. By then they probably have read plenty about how the stock market and overall economy works.

Yet I don't want to assume they have a decade of experience in stock picking behind them. It helps enormously if someone can start their investing journey young. The compounding effect is what is always highlighted by the media. I believe another aspect may be equally important. That is, the younger you start, the mistakes you make have less damaging financial impact. Most of us will always make big mistakes starting out, I know I did. Even if your strategy is just passive index ETFs a young investor can easily panic at the wrong time. Picking your own stocks mean there are countless other ways to make mistakes. Far better you learn from these on a small portfolio in your early 20s, than when you are 40 years old. Or even worse making a big mistake on the eve of retiring in your 60s.

That is why I would like to attempt to write a book on some of my investment strategies that someone young can understand. For example someone with a few years in the workforce and already having tinkered with the stock market and read a few other books on investing themselves. I have no idea whether my son will be interested in active investing in his early 20s, but if he is I can give him this book.

I still think very experienced investors can get something from this book. They may come across a certain strategy that they feel suits their temperament, of which they previous didn't consider.

3) I am worried about the future return prospects on the passive index approach

At the beginning of the year 2020 I thought markets were very expensive. It felt it was becoming pointless for me to keep researching more new stocks for my watchlist. That is the area I normally spend a big part of my week doing.

For instance, what if you want to base your strategy on a diversified set of large Australian Stock Exchange (ASX) stocks? This is what things looked like around January 2020.

Over the last 20 years:

- CSL's average PE is 25.8x – now 40.3x (record high).
- WOW's average PE is 18.06x – now 27.2x (record high).
- CBA's average PE is 13.14x – now 17.2x (record high).
- RMD's average PE is 24.8x – now 37.3x (record high).
- ASX's average PE is 19.69x – now 31.7x (record high).
- MQG's average PE is 13.36x – now 16.5x (10 year high).
- WES's average PE is 12.01x – now 25.7x (record high).
- TLS's average PE is 14.2x – now x (17 year high).
- AMC's average PE is 13.35x – now 16.4x (5 year low).
- ALL's average PE is 19.63x – now 21.8x (three year low).
- COL's average PE is 19.95x – now 23.4x (only been around a year or so).
- BXB's average PE is 17.75x – now 22.3x (10 year high).

Source: https://marcustoday.com.au/

In terms of US markets, throughout 2019 there was virtually no earnings growth within the S&P500 index. Yet that market returned about 30% in the calendar year.

What did common valuation metrics for US shares look like in early 2020?

The CAPE Ratio

This simply measures how share prices look versus smoothing out 10 years of earnings per share (EPS) figures. Many believe this makes more sense than simply examining prices versus last year's EPS. Also it may make more sense than trying to use the forward P/E ratio, which estimates EPS figures in the future. After all, we see in finance how so many forecasts are unreliable. Below would indicate this market has never been more expensive over the last 70 or so years, except around 1999.

Cyclically-adjusted P/E (CAPE) at 90th percentile

SOURCE: Haver Analytics, Goldman Sachs Global Investment Research. As of December 31, 2019.

The market *cap-to-GDP measure* is one that Warren Buffett used to hint that US stocks were at lofty levels in 1999. A bear market later started in the year 2000 that saw that market almost half in value.

Now in 2020 it looks worse than back then.

US equity market cap-to-GDP ratio at all-time high

SOURCE: Haver Analytics, Goldman Sachs Global Investment Research. As of December 31, 2019.

But this is explained by the increased relevance of foreign earnings from great US companies these days, so it should be high versus US GDP right? In other words, why compare companies with a heap of foreign earnings to a GDP figure of one single county like the US?

I am not so sure about that excuse.

Exhibit 1: Foreign Sales as a Percentage of Total Sales

2018	2017	2016	2015	2014	2013	2012	2011	2010	2009	2008
42.90%	43.62%	43.16%	44.35%	47.82%	46.29%	46.59%	46.14%	46.29%	46.57%	47.94%

Source: S&P Dow Jones Indices LLC from data provided by S&P Global Market Intelligence. Data as of July 2019. Past performance is no guarantee of future results. Table is provided for illustrative purposes.

If you believe that though you must take a look at the above table. Foreign earnings as a percentage of sales are less relevant than around a decade ago. A decade ago this market capitalisation to GDP ratio was at a more normal level. So what justifies it exploding higher in recent times?

But interest rates are so much lower I hear you say?

Well what do low rates say historically about future share price returns?

Unfortunately the data tells us the lower that real interest rates are, the worse future return prospects are for equities! Check out the below chart.

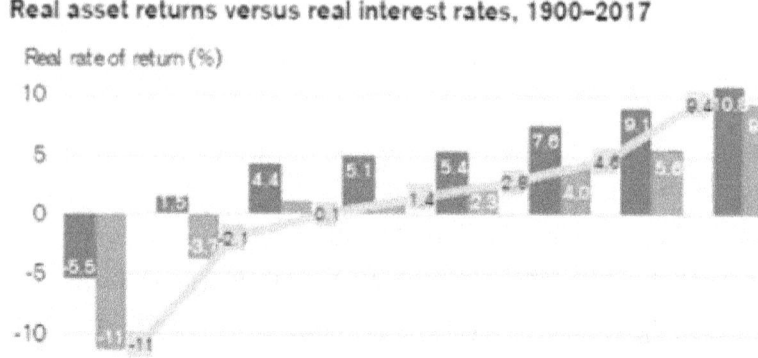

Source: Elroy Dimson, Paul Marsh, and Mike Staunton, DMS dataset

I am not surprised. Consider that equities were a great generational buy in the early 1980s. Not because interest rates were low, but because they were very high! The market was overjoyed in the next decades as interest rates eventually moved down. Can we experience such enthusiasm in the future? Remember the starting point is now about the lowest rates we have seen virtually ever, in 5,000 years or so?

Another point on interest rates. If the US market CAPE ratios, market capitalisation to GDP measures can flirt with record highs due to low interest rates, why don't we see this with other markets? Europe and Japan are not experiencing similar enthusiasm.

Most of the arguments I hear justifying valuations in the US equity market just strike to me as saying "it is different this time". Those are normally dangerous words when it comes to investing.

Other reasons for writing this book

My son had his first birthday earlier in 2020 and I also thought it is a good stage to spend more time with him. Writing the book is quite a flexible task with time management, rather than promising deliverables to other people. That also suits the fact my son doesn't always agree with how I like to schedule my day's activities. He doesn't sleep at the times I prefer him to sleep! A long term task of writing a book like this is handy to pick up in an ad hoc manner when it suits my time.

Then however a few months later I found myself separated from my son for a long period thanks to the coronavirus travel restrictions! Suddenly I had more spare time on my hands than I imagined. If I was ever to write a small book in my life, this was the ideal time.

There is a reason I have been mentioning FIRE. That is because I see now as an inflection point where certain investing methods will come under question. One such strategy is the passive index ETF strategy that by and large all FIRE investors gravitate to.

I just think that is an important theme to touch on. As this potential trend change can enhance the appeal of using some of my special situation investing strategies.

Then not long after I began writing this book in January 2020, we started to witness a sudden sharp bear market thanks primarily to coronavirus. I thought this would be an ideal time to re-visit my investment strategies to make sure I am sticking with them in such volatile markets. As such a turbulent time evolves my writing could also act as a bit of a diary to reflect upon how I handled my investments.

Why would I give my investing secrets away?

I have noticed a lot of scepticism towards those who blog or write eBooks. I think plenty of that is warranted. The question you should ask of many in the investment industry is their motivations. For example what if you wish to learn from somehow writing about investing? A reasonable question may be from where do they make their money from? If the answer is they make more from their blogging / eBook / courses etc than from their investment portfolio, maybe there is some information in that. It might be worthwhile what you can learn from their marketing abilities rather than their comments about investing.

Personally, I have barely covered my own costs from the blog I started. If I costed out my time then it would be a massive loss maker!

It is also worth asking why those in the investment industry would share any of their strategies? If the information is valuable wouldn't they keep it to themselves? I have pondered this, but I have never considered the investment strategies I will outline as any unique insights from me. They have all been discussed before by other investors far more successful than me. You will find on amazon many other books about special situation investing. If I supply yet another book on the topic I hardly think it well get popular enough to crowd out opportunities in the stock markets! These inefficiencies in markets that I attempt to exploit have gone on for decades and will likely continue to do so.

One benefit of sharing knowledge as is sometimes the favour is returned even more so. When I have done this via blogging it has been a pleasant surprise that smarter investors have made contact with me. This can be helpful when investing in small companies at it is difficult to keep on top of all the opportunities.

Some other shareholders have also got in touch and been helpful in getting a message delivered to the management of companies when necessary. I hope after reading this book that you will subscribe to my blog at valueinvestingforalivng.com if you haven't done so already. It will always be free to look. I say this only because I think large groups of smaller shareholders can play an increasingly important role in driving shareholder activism in the future. I think it can be beneficial for likeminded investors to remain in contact in that regard. Especially when considering the potential to influence corporate governance matters with ASX Listed Investment Companies (LICs).

In short I am writing this to help gather my own thoughts on my strategies. When forced to write for the public it forces you to be far more thorough in outlaying the reasons for your decisions. I hope by the time I have finished writing I will gain more of a perspective on where I should be looking to improve my methods.

As discussed, I also want to see if I can convey my strategies to relatively inexperienced investors.

So why buy this book then when there are already plenty of special situation investing books out there!? Well it gives another personal story as to how someone else has used the strategies relatively successfully. I have also tied it in with how this type of investing compares with passive index investing and aiming for FIRE.

Some books written by investors managing tens of millions of dollars are not as relevant. They can be too large to buy some of the stocks I play around in at times. This book is also more relevant for those interested in the closed end fund market. More specifically, those who are curious how I have applied the strategies to the Australian Stock Exchange, and in many cases the closed end funds there known as Listed Investment Companies (LICs). It can still be just as relevant for investors in other global markets. I have also invested on quite a few different global exchanges over the years.

Other strategies for FIRE

I haven't spent much time discussing the FIRE community on my blog. I do realise though there are plenty of readers from my traffic sourced from google that would be aiming for FIRE. One reason for writing this book is because of the dozens of related FIRE blogs I see, I rarely come across active investors.

Firstly, let me clarify that is actually a good thing. I believe the majority should stick with index ETFs in pursuit of such goals. (although perhaps temper their return expectations, given market valuations as I just discussed). However I also believe we shouldn't be too close minded of alternative methods. After all, do we in other areas of life consciously aim to achieve the "average" result? This is what we are settling for with index ETFs (not that there is anything wrong with that!). That can make sense of course, as the risk of trying to gain above average may result in us doing far worse than average. Then again that is the same with many other aspects of our life. Do we settle when we see an "average" job become available to us as there is a risk we may not find a better one? Do we settle for an "average" husband or wife to live with, because there is a risk of not finding a better one? Some probably do in both examples but I am sure some don't!

CHAPTER 2 - Why take an active approach?

A lot should come down to how much time and effort we can put in to achieve better than average results. Most investors are simply not interested in spending many hours researching investments. For those that way inclined, I don't really want to suggest you rush in to try the strategies in this book. You would likely end up with poor results if the passion isn't there. This book is more suited for those that find themselves regularly wanting to read about the share market during their free time. Or perhaps those who have accepted that passive index investing is the only way without any thought of alternative methods. It can help to have an open mind. Even if it results in you deciding to stick with an ETF strategy, it could be helpful.

I would now like to bring up some points that I feel are often overlooked. Points that could favour a more active investing approach for those trying to achieve FIRE.

1) You don't incur high actively managed investment fees - One of the big failures of managed funds are due to high fees. In using a DIY actively managed approach you are not leaking out management fees and all sorts of other fees and costs. What deters a lot of investors in having a go at managing their own portfolio is the well-publicised "SPIVA" reports scorecards. This is research published by S&P Dow Jones Indices that show a very high percentage of fund managers underperform over the long term. They assess the fund's returns after some hefty fees taken out. Fees on actively managed products are often likely to hamper returns by more than 1.5% per annum if you are a retail investor in Australia. That is a handy head start a private investor has when they embark on trying to beat the benchmark.

2) Technology has made the task more accessible – These days you have access to all the company announcements online at your disposal. The information disparity that existed between retail and institutional investors has closed a lot. Same with trading costs, which used to be very high for a small investor decades ago.

Now you can stay well informed from anywhere in the world. Download company announcements, presentations, conference calls etc. Filter through the market and rank stocks by P/E ratio, yield, price to book, whatever takes your fancy. Google other opinions on stocks, macro and micro influences. Access some of the better investors thoughts regularly on Livewire markets or twitter, the list goes on.

3) To even be contemplating FIRE arguably shows you are a few steps ahead of the population to begin with - To identify at a young age that FIRE might be possible arguably might mean you are brighter than most to begin with. At least somewhat equipped to apply a slightly active approach with a genuine chance of beating the benchmark. (given the inherent advantages a smaller investor has over the institutions, which I shall later elaborate on).

4) Extra time available when achieving FIRE - If you get to the FIRE stage you will have more available time in the week that can be spent doing investment research. If you are ok with that of course. This can eventually become a significant edge over others you are transacting with in the market.

5) Tax efficiency - A DIY investing approach gives you must better control of after tax returns. Life changing tax efficient gains in the market can be achieved when you invest in a successful individual company and there is no need to sell. CGT can be postponed for decades or indefinitely. It becomes effectively like having interest free debt from the government in comparison to having sold.

Open ended funds are unlikely to take advantage of such situations. The pressure from outside investors is likely to motivate them to take profit at times. Redemptions can effectively force this. Even if it is a closed end fund they may also be constrained by caps on position or sector sizes. That may result in them selling early and paying tax.

6) You are not really taking on the professionals at their own game - Some discourage you from actively managing your money by making the scary point that you are taking on the brightest and most professional investors at their own game. This is not entirely true as it is very rare that the so called professionals get to play the game they like. All sorts of agency issues exist, which I shall cover in a bit more detail shortly. They all mean most professionals can't act like professional long term investors. You can.

So what do I mean but saying all sorts of agency issues exist? Firstly, studies have shown many fund managers have very little "skin in the game", i.e. they don't always place their own hard earned into the managed fund in question. Increasingly we are finding that employees these days are switching jobs far more often. This means more fund managers are concerned over the performance of their funds over the next 3-5 years maximum rather than looking at a longer term horizon. You of course don't have that issue when managing your own portfolio. For the professionals that can't look well beyond a few years, they are likely to chase shorter term trends which is not ideal.

It is not just the portfolio manager's fault for taking the short term view. The reality is history has shown the clients somewhat force them on this. Investors in funds will not usually have the patience to stick it out for the long haul and give them the chance to think very long term.

Fund managers are not only concerned about picking the right stocks, but also that plenty of funds come in the door to invest with them. This gives them a bias to invest in and discuss stocks in their reporting that might appeal to the public. Such stocks may not necessarily represent the best investments. They may represent a good form of advertising to boost their assets under management (AUMs). If they don't have skin in the game then they are better off trying to grow AUMs this way. This encourages them to invest in whatever companies are well known and popular with the public, often past success stories. However the more attractive investments on a risk / reward basis may lie in unpopular areas, which they avoid.

Professional fund managers are also prone to suffer from herd like behaviour, what I think of as "career risk". Some say that if you are going to be wrong in your forecasts, make the same mistake everybody else is making! You won't get sacked that way. You can point the finger and say that there were other credible analysts doing the same thing. The problem is this thinking once again creates a bias to hunt for popular stocks and pay high prices as a result.

When fund managers have established a great historical record and got plenty of inflows, it can cause them to start to hug the index. For example if they suddenly have a superb 5 year record, this is a great selling point in the industry for likely the next few years. The temptation might be there to start reducing risks in terms of the benchmark, i.e. stop doing what delivered the good results in the first place! Since the employees may not be thinking they will necessarily be there past the next 5 years, why not just capitalise on the past? Start to mirror the benchmark more, where you know the performance table will still look relatively attractive. Then just concentrate on advertising the historical record. That may suit the fund managers, but not you as an investor!

Even the reverse scenario may pose a significant problem for you as an investor. If the fund manager has a terrible historical record, perhaps they will try to gamble their way out of it! Of course you probably wouldn't try this with your own money. Yet the fund manager might think they don't have much to lose. For example if they were not invested in the fund, they could just think the product will get shut down and forgotten about. The fund manager might still get another decent job or just start up a different style of fund if the gamble doesn't pay off. No major problem, for them anyway.

Then there is the general pressure of poor performance that leads to redemptions from clients and forced selling. There can be trading costs due to substandard liquidity in the underlying investments needed to sell to fund redemptions. A private investor shouldn't have to contend with this, well assuming of course your husband or wife doesn't pressure you the same way!

Issues such as above are important to keep in mind before completely believing those that tell you the smart money can never beat the market. Reading above you can understand a lot of the funds management industry cannot behave in such a smart way due to these agency issues. It is therefore not really the "smart money".

You of course, have none of the above problems that regularly lead to underperformance from the professionals.

7) Wide investing opportunity set. - From what I have seen FIRE investors are rarely looking at getting to stock portfolios of over $5 million. Consider this Warren Buffett quote on how size can impact performance, *"If I was running $1 million today, or $10 million for that matter, I'd be fully invested. Anyone who says that size does not hurt investment performance is selling. The highest rates of return I've ever achieved were in the 1950s. I killed the Dow. You ought to see the numbers. But I was investing peanuts then. It's a huge structural advantage not to have a lot of money. I think I could make you 50% a year on $1 million. No, I know I could. I guarantee that."*.

This is a huge advantage you have over the average managed fund. This is another advantage that rarely gets mentioned in books that push the retail investor towards passive index investing. Professional fund managers would be very jealous of someone being able to get their performance figures off such a modest pool of capital. They would love to invest in many of the small stock opportunities that are available to you, but not to them due to size.

It can be challenging to start a funds management business these days with much less than $100 million in AUMs. It is not as economic as many perceive with all the increasing compliance costs. Client usually expect some depth in the number of investment team members. Also the expectations are increasing in terms of the transparency you need to provide in terms of client reporting. The costs can add up.

If a fund manager is operating with $100 million in AUMs it makes it challenging to invest in companies with a market cap of under $100 million. A relatively "concentrated" position size might be considered 5% of the fund if they were bullish on a stock. Therefore in this example they would need to acquire 5% of the entire company. This is often unrealistic, at best it might take months or even years to do. Obviously it can vary a lot.

A private investor is however likely to be able to buy the same stock very easily to get to 5% of their own investment portfolio. For this reason these small stocks are often under researched. The fund manager may decide to avoid conducting research on the stock altogether if liquidity doesn't look sufficient. The stock broking side finds it uneconomic to bother providing research on such a company. That can mean the investors on the other side of the trade might be retail investors. Hopefully though you are putting a bit more time and effort into it than them, and you therefore have a significant edge. The trend of smaller companies not being under research coverage from brokers and fund managers is only going to grow. This is due to the increasing popularity of passive index investing over the last decade. Such a trend pushes money towards larger stocks and away from small stocks.

You also don't have to set limitations as to the overall construction of your portfolio. A fund manager is trying to design a product that appeals to a huge number of different individuals. That will lead them to put all sorts of constraints to please everyone. This may include single stock limits, sector limits, geographic limits, limits on percentage held in cash, etc. These days more funds are trying to appeal by adding restrictions for ethical reasons. Not all of these ethical slants will agree with your values.

When it comes to managing your own portfolio, you do you! A lot of those restrictions I highlighted can also contribute to the professionals underperforming.

8) You only need a few good stock ideas a year – At first glance the prospect of managing your own portfolio can look like a full time job! Now I concede at times personally I have almost made it into one in recent years, but that is by choice. When you break it down, it may not necessarily have to be as time intensive as you first think.

Let's remember my previous point about not having any constraints in terms of the construction of your portfolio. You, unlike plenty of fund managers, are also not forced to have an opinion on key stocks in a particular benchmark. Fund managers in Australia often need a team of analysts just to think about which of the four major banks offers the best value just to begin with.

Whilst many funds may own between 50- 100 stocks, you could achieve a huge amount of diversification by owning around 20. Even more so in my opinion than the popular ASX200 index. This index is heavily concentrated in sectors such as banks, financials and resources.

So don't feel you have to analyse 100 companies and dissect every announcement they make daily every year! If you uncover even less than 20 good ideas that can easily be enough. That may still sound daunting. Remember though you don't even have to hold 20 companies straight away. There is nothing wrong with easing yourself into the process. For example starting with half a dozen or so of your picks and holding some index ETFs for a while.

I would also argue that if you can uncover some ASX LIC opportunities at good discounts, 20 holdings could be overkill. Remembering that the LIC itself may hold dozens of different companies within it. This book discusses ASX LICs more in later chapters.

When you break it down to such a level, it might mean that you only need to uncover less than a handful of good stock opportunities in a year. When your portfolio is set up, it can be far less time intensive. Finding another stock to buy might also only need to occur a few times in the year. I am assuming with this approach you have a bias to select stocks you think can be held for a very long time, which is far less time intensive. Some of my strategies can be shorter term in nature, but by no means all of them. Thus how many hours a week you are prepared to devote to all this can be controlled to a certain extent by the portfolio turnover you aim for.

Investors who set out with a goal to have a low portfolio turnover can enable themselves well to stick within their circle of competence. You can devote plenty of time to research fewer companies, ones that you understand well. It can also be very tax effective if you have the skill of finding stocks you can stick with for the very long term.

9) You aren't as worse off as you think compared with the professionals in terms of your research time and ability – Despite all of what I said in the last point, you still may feel daunted by how the professional fund managers have large teams of analysts. I would just like to point out though that they don't always have the extent of time on their hands as you may think.

Increasingly they are getting dragged into the distractions of issues such as compliance, operations, client reporting, marketing etc.

Sometimes the key thesis for owning a stock can be the simple observations we make in everyday life. Your or I are just as equipped in that respect as the professional fund manager. This theme was made famous in the Peter Lynch book "One Up On Wall Street". In fact, you may even be better equipped on the basis you spend more time with the "common folk" than the fund manager who could be making circa half a million in salary! Most of the economic forces revolve around the average consumer. The more in touch with this demographic and can understand them, the better edge you will have.

Although you won't have a team of analysts to work with yourself, this is not always a disadvantage for you. It can be quite difficult sometimes for funds management teams to agree on investment decisions. This has the potential to bring about an overall lack of conviction from the fund manager and lead to underperformance. You don't have to convince anyone about your investments apart from yourself.

There is also nothing stopping yourself from tapping into a network of another investors to exchange ideas. I wouldn't recommend blindly copying anyone before doing your own extensive research. However there is nothing wrong with getting the idea to start researching a stock based on a discussion you have had with another investor. This can be a way to leverage off extra intellectual capital like what funds management teams try to create themselves. This is a lot easier than decades gone by due to technology and various forms of social media.

10) Aiming for FIRE is already unrealistically trying to do something beyond what the average person achieves. Why not take this mindset to beating the market's average return? - Achieving FIRE by definition is very difficult, since overwhelmingly most don't manage to retire early. There is a risk in setting this FIRE goal but not getting there. One risk might be you have sacrificed some enjoyment in the shorter term by tightening your belt with expenditures.

Do we give up on this difficult goal due to such risks? Many pursuing FIRE would say no.

Should we give up on the difficult goal of trying to beat the market's average because most fail? Well many in the FIRE community would answer yes to this.

Both are difficult achievements. I don't think all those pursuing FIRE should automatically rush into the conclusion active investing is not worth it on this basis. Seems a little inconsistent to me this thought process.

Having said that, those that want a simple method and not spend hours a week thinking about stocks, for sure go passive.

Chapter 3 - Some weaknesses of the passive index ETF approach

Once again, as I will do throughout this book, I emphasise that the passive index ETF approach is still likely the most suitable strategy for most investors. I just like to bring up some of the weaknesses, because I feel they haven't been given enough attention in the media. Due to the success of the passive index approach over the last decade many newer investors might be oblivious to the negatives.

1) Behavioural - It may not be as easy as you think. Consider this, using the passive index ETF approach will basically get you "market returns". The main variable on this will be the extent to which the retail investor does harm by trying to time the market. On this basis the stats are not good! Many studies have been made how investors pile in and out of asset classes at the wrong time. That is, the return investors get on open ended funds are far inferior to the returns published by such funds, for this reason.

Is it therefore logical to expect on average we can use index ETFs to get the historical share market performance? You may answer that by saying I have more of an ability to stick with the investment strategy than most, so it is different for me. How different is that to a private investor saying they can beat the benchmark because their ability to stick to a strategy is better than most? The FIRE community strangely dismisses trying to beat the equity benchmarks because on average most fail. Yet they are still happy to set a goal to FIRE, even though clearly most fail. They are also happy to try to stick to a strategy over decades, even though the stats say the average investor fails at this.

This type of study is performed by www.dalbar.com, and below I have taken a few charts that illustrate the results from their 2017 study.

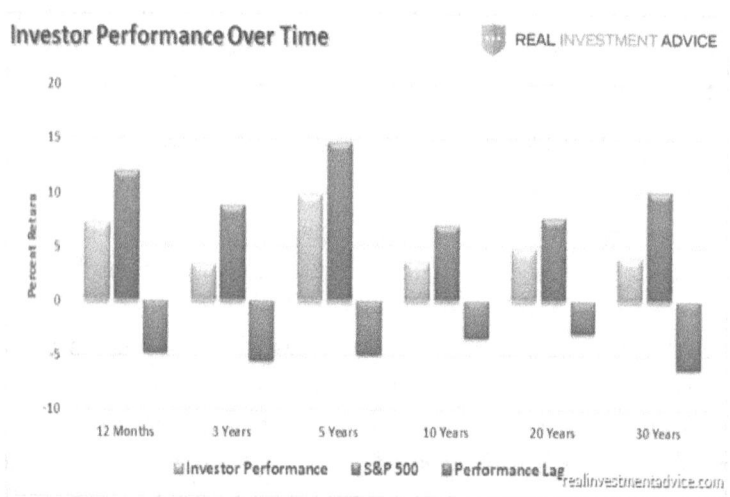

Now some may correctly pose the question to me why I am using a study based off actively managed funds and projecting conclusions onto passive indexed ETFs?

Well the same study also showed it is not fees that are driving this underperformance. Refer to below.

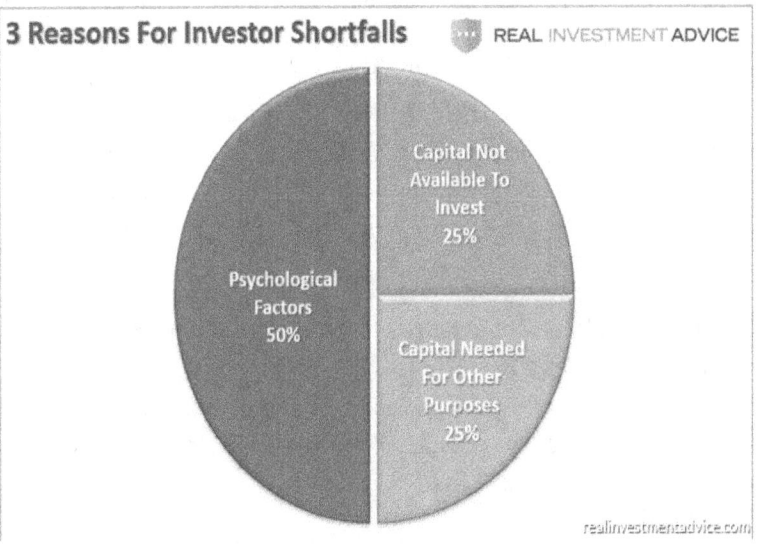

The above reasons are just as relevant when it comes to investing in passive index ETFs.

Don't get me wrong, I am not suggesting these reasons do not also apply to people actively managing their own portfolios. Clearly they do. I am just making the point that the FIRE community instantly assumes anyone participating in investing in passive index ETFs rightfully is assured of getting the benchmark return. Although it may seem a "simple" approach, it is not easy to implement.

Decisions are still required on asset allocation even when using index ETFs. (More on that next). Behavioural biases will arguably lead investors to overweight countries at their peaks and underweight them when they are at their cheapest.

2) What is the right benchmark, all these "passive" decisions are still active? Should it be all US because it has been one of the best stock markets historically and captures a lot of multinational companies? Should we include more China as it is such a huge part of global GDP, compared to a relatively low weighting in global indexes? If I live in Australia should I invest considerably in this for tax reasons, or currency reasons? The list of questions can go on and on.

There are still heaps of active decisions to make within what is often described as a passive strategy. This means there are also heaps and heaps of tempting decisions and reasons to alter the mix along the way. That results likely in further potential value erosion for reasons like I made in point 1.

3) Popular real return assumptions are unrealistic? - 4% is a popular rate of return to expect to hear from those pursuing FIRE i.e. perhaps save up 25 times your annual budget. This is not as easy to implement on index ETFs like most have you believe. Such a rule stems mainly from discussion of US markets over a century or so of data. If we are going to use such long periods of data to reach a conclusion, we must consider what things were like in the early part of the 20th century. Basically this means many have cherry picked one of the best markets in the world in hindsight to arrive at certain conclusions. In reality, a century or so ago it was not clear that to invest in US markets was the way to go. As I am from Australia, the same argument applies there also. Australia happens to be one of the best markets in the world over the last 100 odd years. Yet I strongly doubt before this time period began that many would advocate placing all their investments in this market. Or the US for that matter.

Some of the best research on such long term data can be seen by reading the annual Credit Suisse global investment returns yearbook.

https://www.credit-suisse.com/about-us-news/en/articles/news-and-expertise/global-investment-returns-yearbook-201902.html

Some points to note are the following. This is how the mix of stock markets looked some 120 years ago compared to now.

Figure 10: Relative sizes of world stock markets, end-1899 (left) versus start-2019 (right)

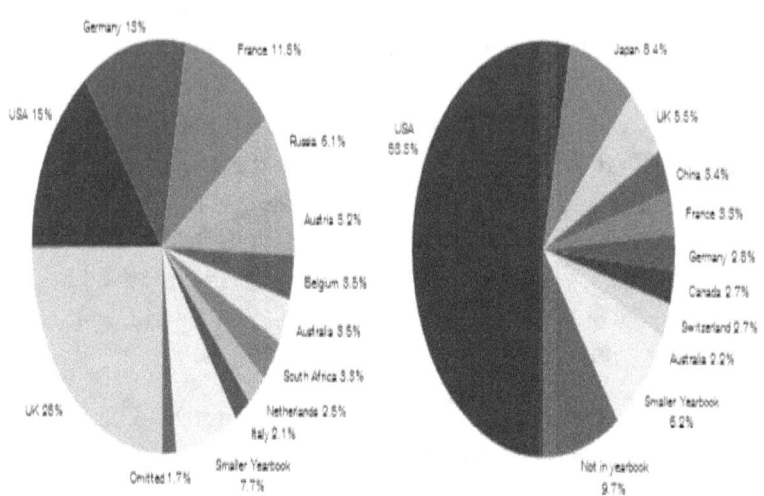

Source: MSCI, FTSE Russell, S&P, Elroy Dimson, Paul Marsh, and Mike Staunton. Not to be reproduced without express written permission from the authors

The U.S. market was just 15%, compared to around 55% now. It made up less of the world compared with the UK which was then about 25%. The 15% exposure to US was similar to that of Germany at 13%.

So when creating rules that imply future returns at certain levels, why do we tend to cherry pick the real returns of the US and Australia? These top performing markets returned about 6.5% real returns. One reason the FIRE community cherry picks the leading country returns is probably because it makes achieving FIRE seem easier. That is, the returns from the UK and Germany of 3% and 5% respectively don't sound as great.

Taking a global look at things at best it appears we should be thinking of returns about 1.5% lower than Australia and the U.S. i.e. real equity returns of 5% rather than 6.5%.

The key conclusion at the start of the Credit Suisse 2019 study was that when rates are low, expected returns should be lower in the future.

So before we get excited over the 6.5% after inflation returns on shares that the media likes to highlight, don't forget some other key points.

It seems more logical to take the 5% real return over many global markets, rather than cherry pick the US or Australian markets.

However even this 5% assumption makes no allowances for:

1) Taxes.

2) Transaction costs.

3) Management fees (admittedly can be kept very low with ETFs these days though).

4) Cash drag – some of your investment portfolio or "target FIRE amount" will likely be left in cash, that will probably earn next to nothing.

5) Likely behavioural weaknesses that erode returns for the average investor. Remember my earlier points on this topic.

6) Potentially reduced returns going forward as real interest rates are very low / negative. Historically this is a bad sign.

7) Investing in a global index ETF will see more than half go to the US market. On so many valuation metrics the US is carrying extremely high valuations. I briefly touched on this issue earlier. This implies significantly lower future returns than we have seen historically.

I will concede that points 5 to 7 might be perceived by some as not to affect them personally. They may be confident of sticking to the strategy. They also may argue that "it's different this time". By that I mean some of my subjective assumptions in terms of current valuation, real interest rates, and what they may imply to future returns.

Still, arguably even points 1-3 alone could take that 5% real global equities return to below 4% anyway. Remembering that many trying to achieve FIRE are targeting saving 25 times their annual budget and hoping not to draw down the capital.

If one tries to be more conservative and instead of just under 4% or so, tries to base their plans on real returns of 2-3%, that can make for a much higher savings goal amount!

Suddenly the temptation for some to try and eke out a slightly higher return through DIY active investing is understandable. Perhaps some simply can't make the goal amount work if it is based on a 2-3% real return rate, should they then give up? I know I wouldn't have quit my full time job at 42 years old if I stuck to index ETFs.

Finally I would like to take a big picture view if it intuitively necessarily makes sense to base your investing mirroring a benchmark.

When an overwhelmingly majority of the market's activity was based on active investing, a reasonably efficient price discovery mechanism existed.

As passive investing slowly takes over from the active amounts, the market is becoming less efficient. The majority of funds flowing into the market will be those giving little or no thought as to valuations they are paying for businesses.

Take a look at the below chart.

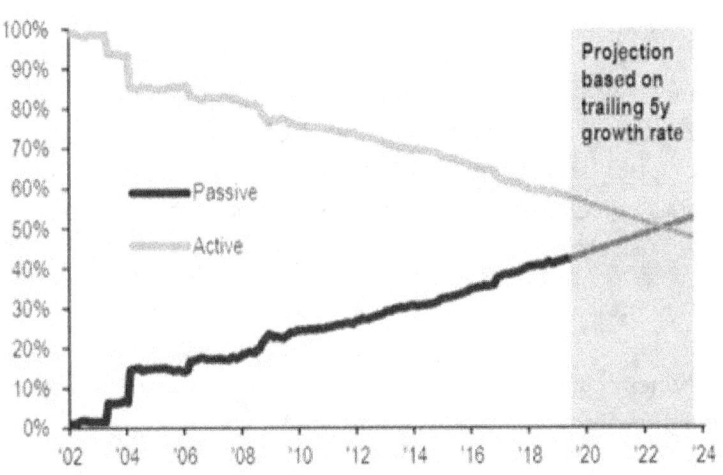

Chart 3: Passive equity fund assets will surpass active by 2022

Source: BofA Merrill Lynch Global Investment Strategy, EPFR Global

Some argue that charts such as above ignore participants in the market such as private investors, pension funds, business holdings etc The argument is that these groups also are big players in the mix that actively enhance price discovery and market efficiency.

My contention is that those players are not good guides in buying stocks based on well researched valuation philosophies. After all, studies have indicated that households follow the herd and contribute mostly into funds towards the end of bull markets. Then are seen redeeming during bear markets!

I therefore prefer to use the chart I have above, separating active versus passive flows in this manner. Yet I actually suspect this overestimates the amount of "genuine" active money in the market.

I believe even a significant portion of the active money are taking positions in stocks with absolutely no consideration as to the prices they are paying. That is because of the pressure of not drifting too far away from the official benchmarks. Remember the earlier points I made about agency issues, performance risk, career risk etc.

Does it intuitively make sense to let your money blindly flow into stocks with very little efficient price discovery? Where an overwhelming number of participants have set the prices with no thoughts whatsoever about valuations?

Remember that the index way to go is driven by historical returns in the market that was entirely different to today. This 4% rule was largely from data when the prices of stocks in the benchmark was almost entirely determined by price discovery from professional active managers. Not the case now. Have a look in the above chart the role passive funds played only less than 20 years ago, compared with today.

Weaknesses of the S&P500 benchmark itself

Whilst the makeup of the S&P500 index is rules based, the media doesn't give a lot of attention that these rules can be tinkered with by a small committee. The rules can therefore by quite subjective. You could argue this "passive" index has its own sort of active tilt behind it.

Some tinkering that has occurred for example, is requiring a certain percentage of the company's shares being available for trade by the public. So if you have a great company with a large founder stake that sits on their core holding, such a company can be underrepresented in the benchmark. Such traits are often considered very good for return prospects.

In the early 2000s they kicked out foreign companies from the index. Suddenly a few years ago REITs got shoved in the index which meant investors were selling other stocks to make room for them. Such tinkering can mean ETFs that track the index have to incur capital gains taxes in order to mirror such moves. The tinkering also distorts the view that the relevant passive index ETFs are necessarily an accurate reflection of historical returns. For instance some of these powerful foreign companies made a great contribution to the past performance. Of course then those wanting more of a foreign flavour to diversify may then have to buy a different ETF mirroring a different index. Who stands to benefit from all this?

The cynical view is such tinkering is purely an attempt to create as much liquidity in the benchmark as possible. This is in order to accommodate the growth of the ETF industry and fee revenue they collect. Bear in mind that the index committee certainly don't care about creating rules to help the performance of those investing for FIRE!

Is the last century or so really a long history to base our assumptions off?

When deciding to invest passively to match an index, our returns are in the hands of the "overall market". Many are happy with this based on data analysis from around 1900.

Whilst this seems like a long period of time at first glance, obviously in the history of the world it is not. I don't have a strong opinion on whether it is a good data set to base your future return assumptions on. Yet to remove the responsibility of picking your own businesses to invest in and choose to be exposed to the overall market, you need some faith in this data. You need to believe the next few decades or so will act in a similar fashion.

I think this is a reasonable assumption but how confident can we be?

Some questions I wonder about this are the following.. I must admit I don't know the answers, but these are thoughts on my mind. As passive indexed investing will test your resolve at certain points, you don't want doubts appearing in your mind *after* the market has halved in value! So here are some of the doubts straight up front just to be prepared.

Has the 20th century had a few tailwinds for investment returns? Will they be there in the future?

- Increasing population, this is the biggest one in my opinion.
- Growing faith in capitalism
- Growing faith in democracies
- Improving peace around the world
- Lowering of corporate tax rates and transaction costs for investors over time

Obviously, this could also be a concern for those wanting to actively manage their own portfolios. But for better or for worse, you will have more control over whatever results you get. Rather than you future determined by the markets as a whole. This may or may not of course turn out to be a good thing! Just some food for thought.

Chapter 4 - Why my strategies suit me and what have they done for me?

Three key factors are at play when it comes to why I invest the way I do.

1) A passion for investing and the time available to pursue this.
This is necessary in my opinion for anyone who decides to try and outperform passive index ETFs. I shall explore to what extent making the time available may be necessary. Also how a portfolio

structure can be chosen to suit your circumstances in terms of how much time to devote to investing.

2) A modest stable portfolio size and long term horizon. I shall go into a bit more detail about how smaller portfolios will continue to have more of an advantage in the future. The other side to this though is that exploiting such opportunities may at times involve stocks with lower liquidity. It is therefore important to have a stable portfolio size, and not have to be a sudden forced seller.

3) A desire for my portfolio to experience less severe drawdowns in bear markets. There are a range of reasons for this which I shall later explore. We probably should expect a few bear markets in our investing lifetimes where the market falls circa 50%. A lot of investors in passive index ETFs look back historically at the eventual recoveries and declare they are fine with this. It is usually investors though who have never lived through such an event. By that I mean never having had a meaningful amount of their wealth exposed to equities in a severe bear market.

Ok let's now dig into the above three areas and explain a bit more how my investing strategies tie in with the above themes. After I do that I shall end the chapter just with a glimpse of some of my own fund's performance history.

1) A passion for investing and the time available to pursue this.
Thus far in this book I have suggested that an investor with a keen interest in the share market has a decent chance of outperforming. I don't want to come across as suggesting it is easy though.

How much time that is necessary to devote to this is a bit like asking how long a piece of string is. I will admit that since I quit my full time job in 2015, I have devoted a big part of every week looking at investment opportunities. This is just as much out of enjoyment for me as it is in terms of it expecting to pay off financially.

The main point of this section though is for me not to say every investor can outperform by X% per annum. Then that they can do this if they just devote as little as 5 minutes a day of research. I would start to sound like a snake oil salesman with an online FX course to sell.

I just want to point out that even when I was working full time I was getting better results than the market. I certainly wasn't putting in the same effort as I have since quitting my job a few years ago though. I simply didn't have as much time available.

What I will say is that for those with less time on their hands, adapt your portfolio construction to suit. It is still important however that you are passionate about investing and happily putting in a certain amount of extra time to the task.

For me that meant when I was working I had a bias to search for more ASX LICs. It is not a bad starting place to look, and in later chapters I will discuss why they can present good opportunities. What it does mean is that these are usually far less intensive time wise to conduct research on. They also provide a lot more diversification than a single stock idea.

Another method that worked for me when I was busier on other things is to restrict my research on individual companies. I would tend to only research those where a good fund manager had already built a stake. Of course the million dollar question is which fund managers are good? I don't mean blindly copying their ideas. The goal is to identify managers with a similar investing philosophy to yourself. As you read the thesis being presented by many in their monthly / quarterly reporting you might have a shortlist of stock ideas. If time is limited just cross out ones where you are finding it difficult to get a clear understanding of. You can get a sense of the ease of understanding a company well just by skimming through an annual report or two.

Earlier in this book I mentioned you only have to get a portfolio going gradually. ETFs can fill the void as you search. If you are a low turnover investor you don't have to uncover a whole lot of new ideas. By looking at companies where a good fund manager has bought into (obviously noting the price they have paid), this can help with developing a strong conviction. This is crucial when it comes to investing. But only take your lead from other investors when YOU have also researched the company and YOU UNDERSTAND IT.

You also must enjoy the process. I recommend you go through at least a handful of the company's annual reports. Ideally get a feel for years in different parts of the economic cycle, and how the company has tracked versus their promises in previous years.

I think it is crucial to write down detailed notes of every purchase and what your expectations are. This can be in the form of having certain items as a checklist. I won't go into huge detail about this or precise valuation techniques as this will be a book of its own!

A lot of this is more art than science, and developed over trial and error, and learning from mistakes. Hence I recommend you start picking your own stocks as young as possible, when the dollar cost of your mistakes are likely to be small. Or if you start picking stocks later in life, that is another argument in favour of making it a small part of the portfolio at first. For example perhaps only 10-20% for your own stock picks, with the rest in passive index ETFs. Slowly work your way up from there. Maybe you end up permanently still keeping a sizeable exposure to ETFs, it is a very individual thing. Half the battle with investing can be choosing the approach you are most comfortable with , and therefore can stick with it.

Despite spending a lot of my time researching companies, I still strongly prefer a portion of my portfolio to be more diversified. For me that has meant in recent years often having circa 30% of my portfolio in LICs that generally hold larger companies. I think if I had 100% in microcap stocks I have picked myself I would go a bit crazy seeing the portfolio value fluctuate so much. I also wouldn't feel comfortable I had the time to really understand how they are all going. My hair would go greyer, and I wouldn't make the best investment decisions when feeling such extra pressures.

It is also not uncommon for small cap stocks to take a bigger hit during a bear market. Then as the bull market gets going produce higher returns than the indices. That means you run the risks of bigger drawdowns, which I don't like. A good example is to check the performance of many small cap fund managers in Q1 2020. Even the smaller stocks I owned during this period did worse than the benchmarks such as the ASX200. My drawdown however was only about half the losses of the benchmarks. ASX LICs were not as bad as some individual companies that I owned. I suspect it helped that many LICs carried some cash inside of them in and were already were trading at large discounts. I also carried plenty of cash or "cash equivalents" before the bear market. In the next chapter I will later explore the top down portfolio structure I often employ in more detail.

If I can get through the bear market losing a lot less from holding cash equivalents, I find the recovery can be very powerful. The rewards can be enhanced from then on from some of the small cap exposures I may hold. Below is some historical data illustrating this from the US markets. As my style is more of a value investor I am most interested in this table.

Returns From the Bottom of Bear Markets Since 1926

Average

	Large Cap	Small Cap Value
One Year	38.2%	70.7%
Three Years	18.6%	29.5%
Five Years	15.9%	25.0%

Median

	Large Cap	Small Cap Value
One Year	31.2%	42.1%
Three Years	19.0%	29.4%
Five Years	16.4%	25.0%

S&P 500 and Fama French Small Cap Value

3 and 5 year numbers are annualized

Source: https://awealthofcommonsense.com/2020/04/what-happened-to-small-cap-value/

2) A modest stable portfolio size and long term horizon. As smaller investors we have a distinct advantage over open ended managed funds. For example we don't suddenly find that a range of clients wish to redeem 20% of our investable funds. This issue can potentially cause major damage to small cap fund managers. If they don't have the cash available they may become forced sellers of illiquid stocks and send prices lower. To solve this they might sell the more liquid holdings but that leaves them with other problems. They may then be stuck with larger weights to other stocks in which they do not have a high conviction in.

Even if they already have the cash available it can still cause problems. That cash can be extremely valuable with the "optionality" it can have in a sudden sharp bear market. If the cash is already depleted it is very hard to capitalise on situations like the coronavirus led bear market in early 2020. Panic selling around mid-March resulted in some amazing opportunities for those that had cash available.

Small cap stocks can have great potential due to being under researched. This is because it is an area where many smart professionals cannot participate in due to their size. The flipside to this opportunity though is these small stocks can require enormous patience waiting for a catalyst. They also have less liquidity to get out of if you are wrong.

Mitigating such issues are if you are in the situation of being a smaller private investor. Even if those that have as much as $10 million in their portfolio have a distinct advantage over professional fund managers. That is a portfolio size that is still usually far too small for professionals to operate funds attracting outside money.

A smaller private investor can be extremely patient waiting for the catalyst as there are no outside investors to answer to. The liquidity risk is minimised to a large extent as there isn't the risk of outside investors redeeming. Now on this issue I am assuming the private investor can separate off some funds for living costs in a conservative manner. You want a completely separate cash bucket set aside from your investing money that will last for many years.

Another way to alleviate some of the risk pertaining to illiquidity is certain special situation investing examples. I will cover such examples later in the book. I refer to examples such as where the investment thesis is for the returns to come from a liquidity event itself. For example think of takeovers, wind ups, large capital returns, special dividends etc. These don't necessarily require liquidity in the secondary market.

The future looks bright in my opinion for a small active private investor in smaller stocks. I have already discussed how this area is becoming increasingly less researched due to the popularity of passive investing. Another factor in favour I believe is simply that small cap value investing is coming off a terrible period. This has led to fund managers suffering redemptions, exiting the space and driving down valuations further through forced selling. Take a look below at the return differences in the US between small cap value and the S&P500 since 2011.

Remember there is plenty of evidence indicating when measuring over many decades small cap value investing produces excess returns. Checkout the below chart for such evidence.

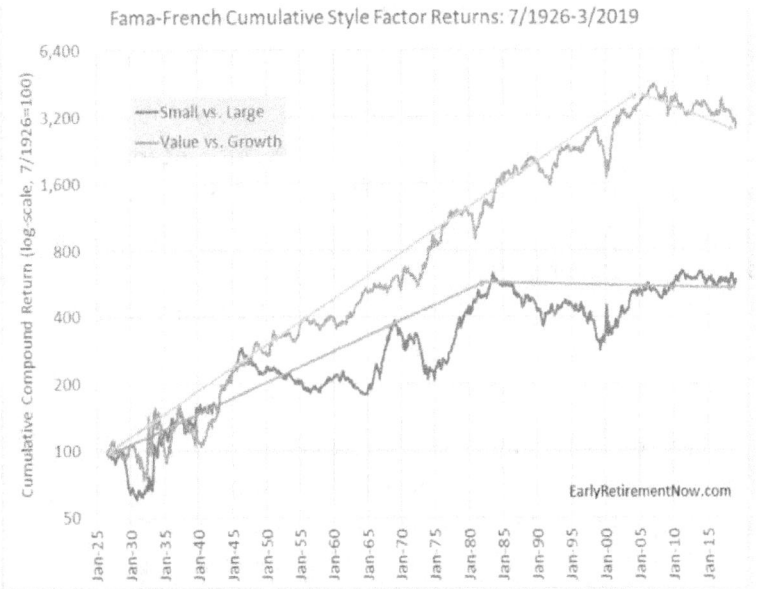

Cumulative (compound) returns of the Fama-French SMB (small minus big) and HML (High book value minus low) factors. Source: Prof. Ken French

No guarantees of course these things work in the future. Yet in my opinion the reason they are likely to work in the future is because it is hard to keep the faith in such factor tilts in your portfolio. Therefore a tough period like the last decade or so might be setting things up for a good outcome going forward.

3) A desire for my portfolio to experience less severe drawdowns in bear markets. First and foremost I prefer shallower drawdowns due to the fact of quitting my full time job in 2015. I think part of the reason I navigated the 2008 bear market well was knowing I had future salary earnings to deploy in the market. Things have changed for me since then so that is the angle I am coming from here. I don't have such a luxury.

If I were only 30 years old or so I would be far more inclined to be closer to fully invested all the time. I would still concentrate on having secure full time employment so I can simply welcome bear markets. Earnings / savings from the next ten years will probably be far greater than the wealth you have amassed at 30 years of age. Therefore far better that a bear market arrives and stays around for years so you can invest those future earnings at good levels.

For those that won't be enjoying a significant boost to free cashflow in the future it can be a different story. From a behavioural point of view I find it challenging to watch my wealth halve in a bear market. This can cloud my mind and result in poor decision making. On the other hand if I carry a decent amount in cash equivalents my mindset changes. I still welcome the bear market and the opportunity to invest in bargains. When you approach things in a positive frame of mind like that you are likely to make better decisions.

This sounds all nice in theory but the logical question from here is won't the excess cash you own drag down your overall returns? I will explore in the next chapter that it is not as much as you think, even if you stuck to passive investing. From personally being an active investor it hasn't been the case at all. I have maintained the advantage of smaller drawdowns, and still gained excess returns over equity indices.

Now some may argue why worry about these 50% drawdowns when the dividends are a lot smoother and we can live on these? I have plenty of sympathy for this view / strategy but strongly caution younger investors about this. It is easy to look back on a chart and a certain market historically and create your own hypothetical how you would have remained calm. We can cherry pick say Australian bank dividends and ignore the performance of many European and US banks. We can ignore the Japan equities experience since 1990 as being different over there. We can tell ourselves that the depression was too long ago to be relevant. Likewise examples of some emerging markets going to zero in the earlier stages of the 20th century.

When you are smack bang in the middle of a bear market, a more modest drawdown to what everyone else is experiencing can be invaluable! Suddenly all your historical charts saying that things should be right may not look as comforting. Especially when at the same time you might be fearing losing your job. Even if dividend flows are only reduced by say 25%, you will be reading on a weekly basis about those predicting greater than 50% falls to your income.

Most investors are vulnerable to panicking amidst such a backdrop. I remember reading posts on forums where sworn long term investors were liquidating portfolios at the lows of the Coronavirus bear market in March 2020. Then within a few weeks were deliberating whether to buy back at 25% higher levels!

Of course there is no guarantee some of the methods I use fixes this problem of panicking. Personally though I find I am less likely to panic when I have had some cash reserves to begin with. Also I worry less if I understand better the businesses I have invested in. As opposed to my investments being in businesses purely on the basis of large crowds gravitating to them in the bull market with no consideration to valuations. (as per the main equity index ETFs – debatable point I realise).

The other thing to note when it comes to the benefits of limiting drawdowns is sequence of return risk. This issue is all captured in the below graph. As the heading suggests, the 3 investors all share factors in common. These are having a $2 million portfolio and the same size $125k annual withdrawals. They also suffered one 25% drop along the journey. The difference is whether they suffered this drop in year 1, year 15, or year 30.

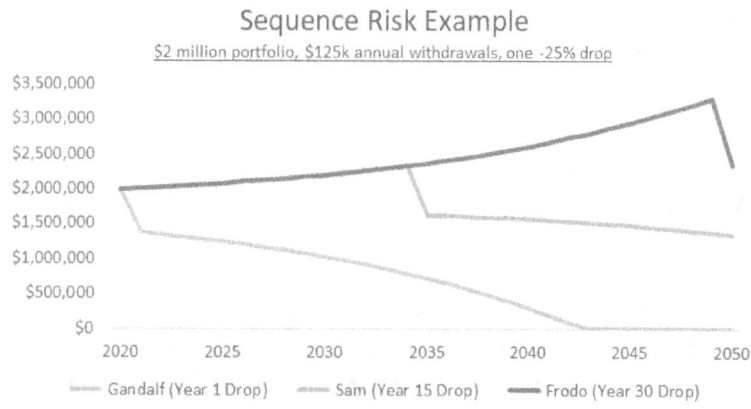

Source: https://movement.capital/one-portfolio-risk-to-rule-them-all/

You can see how a large drawdown in an earlier year makes a huge difference, for the worse! These investors obviously don't have the luxury of ploughing more salary earnings into the market. So once again I highlight the importance as it relates potentially to certain investors. i.e. those that might be soon looking to FIRE, or already retired / semi-retired etc.

Finally I would also like to note that the annualised returns for the US equity markets often leave out an important point. The numbers look good over a century or so I certainly don't dispute that. What is mentioned less though is how "lumpy" the returns can be. It can be hard mentally if you are passive investing because the returns are essentially outside of your control once you decide on a strategy. For example if you go all in the US equities market you need to keep the faith over very long periods when this is seriously tested. We can be talking about 15-20 year periods with little return at all for your strategy. How many passive investors that had the unfortunate experience of retiring at the early stages of one of these phases would keep the faith?

Retiring and going all in with US equities in say 1906, 1929, 1966, or 2000 seriously tested you're staying power!

In many cases there was little to show for your efforts some 10-20 years later. So much for long term investing. Can you sit back in such circumstances and say things will be ok? That the businesses that were chosen for me effectively by the passive index crowd, will all work out for me fine?

My own fund's performance history

Initially I was a bit reluctant to do this for a variety of reasons. I also didn't like the idea of doing it without capturing a bear market. So when I began writing the book this table wasn't going to be in it. I guess though we ticked that box with the coronavirus led bear market starting in early 2020. Although bear in mind the performance for the 19/20 year is still ongoing and unaudited (at the time of publishing this eBook), so the table featured later below is audited to June 30, 2019. Even at April 30th 2020 though at least the outperformance vs the ASX200 has increased. Nominal returns are still above 12% per annum despite the shock of the Coronavirus market falls.

Some might view the returns as poor, some may think they are fabricated. So what does the upcoming performance table represent, and what are the limitations?

- They are for my self-managed superannuation retirement fund (SMSF) since inception in the beginning of the 2014 / 2015 FY. They have been fully audited by external parties and are after all fees and taxes.

- I have been investing in the share markets since 1992 so the table will show nothing of my experience in the earlier years, or from my investing accounts outside of my SMSF.

- I thought it is still a useful snapshot to include in this book for these reasons. It is audited, involves only ASX listed stocks and doesn't experience contributions / redemptions. It also roughly began when I had more time to devote to investing from quitting full time work. These are the same themes I have emphasised in this book, i.e. devote a bit more time, take a long term view on ASX stocks with funds that are not under pressure from unexpected redemptions. It very much closely mirrors the exact strategies I outlay in this book.

- The point in showing this is more to see how the returns are smoother than the equity benchmarks. (Remembering at the time of writing my fund has fallen far less than benchmarks in early 2020). I know some might say the ASX200 accumulation index isn't a good benchmark. I trust others can look up other benchmarks though and see generally my returns compare favourably.

- Here they are then at the time of publishing. No trolling please ☐.Remember I am not trying to start up any snake oil type stock tipping services on the back of this! I just think it is some useful context for this book, and that excluding this would make this book lacking relevance.

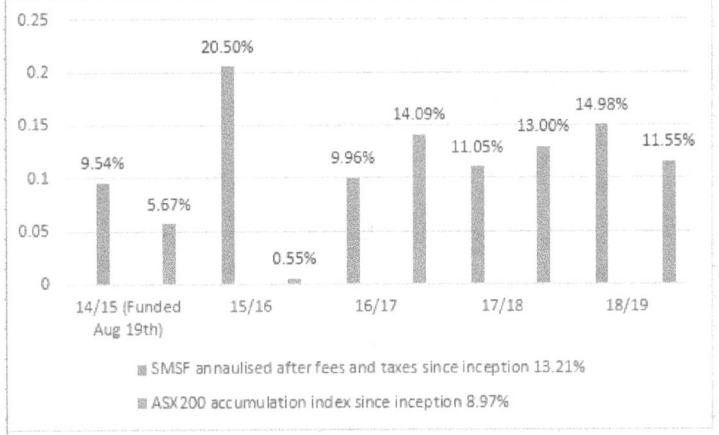

- If someone wants to get in touch though about the details above I am open to that in certain circumstances. I refer to a more professional relationship in the sense of collaborating on individual stock research. So I am open to sharing the more detailed performance audit in that context if needed. Indicative unaudited results nearing the time of publishing (April 30, 2020) are still showing returns since inception of above 12% per annum even after the recent bear market.

- For those that don't think this is worthwhile doing there might be a little more context looking at my user profile on the strawman.com site (username – stevegreenycom). It shows some of the style of trades I have gravitated to. It only is a very loose resemblance though of a small part of my trading over the last few years. I can only say at the time of writing this book it gives a hint of my investing style on trade examples. I can't say for sure whether I will continue being active over on that site or not. Or whether the site stays the same or changes its direction.

CHAPTER 5 - Portfolio construction from a top down perspective

My portfolio construction techniques from an asset allocation point of view are very much related to limiting drawdowns. I think even most investors would understand that the risk of a major drawdown is reduced by having more diversified asset allocations. However the reason plenty would not choose to be more diversified is it logically implies lower returns in the long run. This is because it is widely accepted that being 100% exposed to equities is likely to produce the greatest returns in the very long term. Yet to what extent does a highly diversified portfolio necessarily place a drag on overall returns?

I have noted the link to Meb Faber's website below because a lot of his work describes how I think of things a lot better than I can explain!

www.mebfaber.com

He has written a book titled "Global Asset Allocation" which I recommend. By the way it is normally very cheap to buy and at times he has offered it for free.

To quote from the amazon page "*Our book begins by reviewing the historical performance record of popular assets like stocks, bonds, and cash. We look at the impact inflation has on our money. We then start to examine how diversification through combining assets, in this case a simple stock and bond mix, works to mitigate the extreme drawdowns of risky asset classes. But we go beyond a limited stock/bond portfolio to consider a more global allocation that also takes into account real assets. We track 13 assets and their returns since 1973, with particular attention to a number of well-known portfolios, like Ray Dalio's All Weather portfolio, the Endowment portfolio, Warren Buffett's suggestion, and others. And what we find is that, with a few notable exceptions, many of the allocations have similar exposures."*

Now I probably should provide a bit of a spoiler alert but I would like to share the key takeaways that most would come away with from reading this book. Once again though I emphasise to support the author, have a read and reach your own conclusions. These are the key thoughts I came away with though.

- Asset allocations can be extremely different but if we assume **investors stick to the strategies rigidly over many decades** the end returns are very close to each other. No matter what different initial asset allocation mix you chose, the end result was nearly always within 1% of each other on an annualised basis. This is often less than management fees many in the industry charge!

- The overall returns are nearly always within one per cent of the long run equity returns. Yet instead of the too frequent 50% type falls we see when going "all in" stocks, other portfolios keep drawdowns at under 30%, some significantly under. Sounds like a reasonable trade off?

- We can easily save 1% or so or much more by steering clear of expensive investment products anyway! You could decide to take the above conclusions to form the basis of a low fee ETF strategy then and rip up and throw away the rest of my book. That is quite a reasonable thing to do!

- I personally believe though I can make up that 1% or so that such diversified strategies often lag a 100% equity portfolio over the very long term. I also believe I can further minimise the drawdowns of even the highly diversified portfolios in Meb Faber's book. This is via stock selection employing many of the "special situations" I will later describe. This is often by using the advantages of running a relatively very small sized portfolio compared with the professionals running public managed funds. So maybe don't throw away this book just yet!

- Other key takeaways from the book are **that sticking with the strategy means rebalancing consistently. However whether this is every 6 months, 1 year, 2 years or whatever is not really the key point, just stick with a method all the way through.**

- Given the marginal differences between different asset allocations returns in the long run, investing is a lot about patience, sticking with the strategy, and keeping fees and taxes low. **Sticking with any strategy is difficult, so the good thing about the above points is the flexibility to choose a strategy that makes you feel comfortable. I would argue strategies with less drawdown risk are much easier to stick with over the long term!**

Are my investing strategies consistent with the above philosophies?

Readers now might be scratching their heads thinking that I am not being consistent. That I invest in closed end funds so how is that keeping costs low? I have a higher portfolio turnover than many other investors so how is that keeping taxes low? I don't always rebalance to exactly my original asset allocations so isn't that inconsistent with what I mentioned above? I shall briefly tackle each of these questions to clear up any confusion of where I stand on such questions and other issues.

That I invest in closed end funds so how is that keeping costs low?

It is true that I regularly invest in ASX LICs that could have a high cost structure. In my opinion though the ones I own in many cases I am getting paid to own them as opposed to incurring any fees, let alone high fees. Does that sound bizarre? Let me explain.

The type of situation that I look for might fit the following example of a LIC. A base management fee of around 1%, with a performance fee of 20% of gains above the benchmark with a high watermark. The LIC might be so far behind its watermark the odds of any performance fees over the next 3-5 years are extremely low. The LIC might be trading at a 25% discount and above $500 million in size. It has some activists circling that are ensuring management look after shareholders otherwise they may instigate a vote to wind it up. Management therefore have an on market buyback in place.

Let's now consider with the above example some basic maths and scenarios over the medium term. A reasonably sized LIC has no barriers to potentially shrinking itself through executing the buyback. (It can be problematic for a $50 million LIC for example as soon the fixed cost structure becomes too large). If they buyback 10% of the shares each year at a 25% discount to NTA that will be accretive to the NTA, i.e. boost asset backing per share by about 2.5% per annum without any risk. This will likely far exceed any fees and costs. Thus I would argue this can be far cheaper to own than even owning an ETF with a charge of under 10bps.

In my assumptions there I have not even yet considered the prospect that the NTA discount could be reduced from say 25% to 5% quite quickly. Sentiment can change or a decision could be made to wind it up or convert to an open ended structure. That could mean an additional huge positive return to what the underlying assets do, which is not possible from an ETF that always tracks the NTA. As you can see sometimes supposedly "expensive" closed end funds structures can be extremely cheap to own. If you choose your targets well you are arguably getting paid to own them.

Aside from closed end funds I do not really incur investment fees the way most think about this issue anyway. I do not seek out investing with fund managers unless I can access them at a significant discount to their assets. Aside from that I am performing the funds management duties by myself. Now it is fair to say my own time I use for that is effectively a cost. Personally though this is what I love doing every day so for me I do not view that as incurring fees. For others well I understand it might be different. Perhaps then if I ever felt I was beginning not to enjoy picking stocks myself I would gradually transition to a more time efficient method. For instance, a portfolio entirely from ASX LICs at large discounts and / low fee ETFs.

I have a higher portfolio turnover than many other investors so how is that keeping taxes low?

It is true that selling stocks can incur extra taxes payable, but you are entirely in control of this when managing your own portfolio like I do.

I therefore consider my approach entirely consistent with Meb Faber's observation on the importance of keeping taxes low. The key thing to remember is to **base your decisions on after tax outcomes.** When you outsource the funds management to others in the industry **they are usually basing the decisions on before tax outcomes which can be inconsistent with your objectives.** That is because they are always publishing before tax performance figures for their marketing.

Most would already realise the advantage of "tax harvesting". This is where you have a stock that is showing a loss and that realising such a loss can reduce your tax payable. This might make a lot of sense if you can find a replacement with greater potential.

I am regularly targeting companies with excessive franking credits, existing tax losses on the balance sheet, or due to pay out large capital returns. Such examples are very much consistent with me keeping taxes effectively low, even though I might be turning over the portfolio more than others. An individual investor also can let profits run for a long time if they are sitting on high quality companies in their portfolio. This therefore defers CGT for long periods.

I do not always rebalance to exactly my original asset allocations so isn't that inconsistent with what I mentioned above?

On this issue I would first note that it not absolutely crucial that investors rebalance at exact times to precisely the original targets. This was a conclusion tested in Meb Faber's research. The main concept to grasp is to remain diversified so you are not buying into bubbles at the extremes. The "all weather" type portfolio is designed to help you avoid the big drawdowns that come from being overly exposed to bubble like valuations at the wrong time. Think of Japanese stocks in the late 80s, or US stocks at the end of the 90s (especially the tech sector).

Whilst I do not always rebalance exactly to my targeted weights, I have strict limits as to how loose I will get with this. (more than 10% away from an asset allocation target is quite extreme for me). After all the point of this diversified portfolio strategy is to stop yourself potentially implementing your own market timing based on your gut feel.

Now let's get into the details of what I think about in terms of the top down view when constructing my portfolio?

What are my broad asset allocation targets?

Equities – 35%

Real Estate / REITs – 25%

Commodities / Commodity stocks – 15%

Cash / Cash Equivalents – 25%

How on earth did I come up with my asset allocation targets!?

I find it is quite consistent with the philosophies I outlined from Meb Faber's book, and also the concept of Ray Dalio's "all weather" portfolio.

In terms of the latter, the idea is that your portfolio holds up in many different environments. This helps with the sleep at night factor. Remember I have emphasised that you need to feel comfortable in what you choose as it is important not to deviate from it. My targets are what I feel comfortable with.

Below is an illustrative snapshot about the general concepts of the "all weather" portfolio that I hope is fairly self-explanatory. The various labels illustrate types of market environments that historically we go through. Different environments can have dramatically different effects on returns on different asset classes.

Hence the idea is to have exposures to a diversified mix of asset classes.

	GROWTH	INFLATION
RISING	25% of Risk • Equities • EM Debt Spreads • Commodities • Corporate Spreads	25% of Risk • Inflation-Linked Bonds • Commodities • EM Debt Spreads
FALLING	25% of Risk • Nominal Bonds • Inflation-Linked Bonds	25% of Risk • Equities • Nominal Bonds

In terms of the type of "weather" (e.g. rising growth, falling inflation etc) the markets are experiencing, the asset classes in the boxes illustrate what would normally expect to perform relatively well. The idea is to have similar levels of exposures that can do well in any of the environments.

Further diversification?

It is beyond the scope of this book, and more for higher net worth investors, but I wanted to briefly note here I also believe in owning assets in different jurisdictions. By that I mean the difference is owning say an ETF that might hold European stocks, or actually owning direct stocks within a European country having set up a brokerage / bank account etc over there. After all some say diversification is one of the few "free lunches" that exists with investing and this is taking it to the next level. Realistically though this line of thinking only suits quite high net worth investors and those that perhaps have dual citizenships.

You are essentially achieving some protection from some crazy political decisions within one country. The same comment can apply to trying to achieve more diversification on how instruments are taxed within one country. For instance do not try and make all your gains via unrealised capital gains, or all on dividends, or all on your home, or just within just your retirement fund etc

What exactly do I mean in regard to some of my own asset allocation headings?

Equities – Whilst I specialise in ASX listed stocks, it can often be exposures to markets all over the world. As we know the ASX has so many vehicles whether they are LICs or ETFs that give exposures to so many different countries. I will later discuss briefly how I may tilt my exposures to different geographical areas in the world. I will also mention how I treat my currency exposures. I should note that I do occasionally invest on other global stock exchanges.

Real Estate – For me this could mean real estate directly, not only listed REITs.

Commodities – I have listed 15% above but for me it is rare that all of this exposure would be in commodity equities. Often a fair chunk of this might be in gold and gold ETFs for example.

Cash – You will note I have mentioned this bucket might also include "cash equivalents". Often my 25% or so cash bucket might only have half of this as real cash. This helps limit the drag of low cash returns. "Cash equivalents" can be listed stocks that stand an excellent chance of turning into real cash within a matter of months. This could be from the expectation of a takeover to finalise, a company going through a wind up for example.

The above weights I personally calculate excluding my main property in Australia of which I do not expect I will ever consider selling.

Aside from the above I also have a rule of thumb not to achieve the above mix purely by a selection of 100% individual small company exposures. As I have discussed in earlier chapters private investors can have an edge here, however small caps can be more volatile. Closed end funds can be a preferable way for me to achieve quite a lot of the above mix if discounts are at very wide levels. If I find I hold more than a third oy my portfolio in individual stocks that are very small, this can go against my philosophy to keep drawdown risk low. That is due to their increased underlying volatility.

What tools might I use to choose which global stocks to include?

I want to stress at this point that my portfolio structure is not so rigid that it is strictly derived from a top down approach from these asset allocations. Often if I think about what I would like to own strictly form a bottom up approach it might well come out reasonably close to such asset allocations anyway.

In terms of my equities bucket you will have probably gathered from reasons already explained I have bit of a bias towards small cap value. Also since I have grown up in Australia and followed the ASX very closely all my life there will be a bias there. What I am mindful though of is major valuation signals of various different global equity markets.

In my lifetime there seems to have been a couple of gigantic bubbles that even without hindsight were obvious not to participate in. I refer to the Japanese equity markets in the late 80s and US equities (more so tech) in the later 90s. I do not view avoiding such markets as market timing. It is not a choice of participating in these markets or holding cash. The debate around whether markets are expensive or not often gets distracted about the false assumption that someone has to choose between one countries equity market or cash.

This gets lost in the debate whether the CAPE ratio is a useful tool or not. As I mentioned earlier in the book, the CAPE just smooths out the last decade's earnings to relate it back to share prices. Arguably it is then more useful rather than just going off last year's earnings, or next year's expected earnings. The latter approaches might over emphasise an extreme year. People often criticise the CAPE because they look at investors who sold stocks and went into cash for a couple of years because valuations were expensive. Only to see that valuations got more expensive. That is not how I like to use CAPE as a tool.

I would urge investors to take a very long term view, and tilt some of their equities exposures to markets that are cheap according to CAPE.

Some work that Meb Faber has done indicates this can provide an excellent tailwind to your equity market returns if you think of it in this way. Refer to the below table for an illustration of this.

The "switch" columns are based on exiting US stocks when the CAPE is expensive above 20 and switching into either the 10 year or 30 year bond. Then you switch back to stocks if the CAPE goes below 20 again. Comes out better than when investors think about switching into cash.

But look at the huge tailwind in the "Global CAPE" column. This implies you do not exit equities to go into bonds or cash. You select the cheapest 25% of countries to invest in their share markets according to the CAPE tool, and regularly rebalance to stay in this cheapest quartile.

Summary of Strategies and Assets, 1993 – 2018

	S&P 500	10 YEAR	30 YEAR	SWITCH 10	SWITCH 30	Global CAPE
Total Return	961.64%	414.82%	667.76%	589.48%	1004.91%	3051.23%
Return	9.10%	5.62%	7.58%	7.06%	9.28%	14.05%
Vol	14.22%	7.21%	13.13%	8.65%	12.88%	19.31%
Sharpe -2.55	0.47	0.44	0.39	0.53	0.53	0.60
MaxDD	-50.95%	-10.23%	-25.84%	-24.99%	-23.47%	-39.62%

Source: https://mebfaber.com/2019/01/06/you-would-have-missed-961-in-gains-using-the-cape-ratio-and-thats-a-good-thing/

Whilst I don't run the equities bucket of my portfolio in such a quantitative way, I pay attention to which global markets are showing up as cheapest in terms of CAPE. This I think is very handy to keep in the back of your mind. Especially when certain ASX LICs might have strong global tilts to particular markets and trade at big discounts.

How do I manage exchange rate exposures?

In this section I do not want to imply I take major views on the directions of various currencies.

I will just say consider your own lifestyle and particular circumstances. I am somewhat of a regular global traveller / nomad in some respects. I therefore make sure I have a big part of my portfolio that benefits from a falling AUD. This is usually even more than half of my investments, but this may not suit others. In my case I have more of my expenditures outside of Australia compared to most.

As a rough rule of thumb though, I believe that it might be quite appropriate for many Australians to have circa 30-50% of their portfolio in global investments that are unhedged. i.e. benefit from a declining AUD. I would think of those percentages as a percentage of one's overall net worth though, i.e. including all assets such as your own home.

There are issues I find many Australians forget about when they decide to have all their investments in AUD. The same theme can apply to residents of other countries and their "home country bias" as it is known.

That is, if you go "all in" with investing in your own country, you can be hit hard in many ways. If your country suffers from major economic problems compared with the rest of the world think of how events may evolve. If the share market and real estate markets in your own country dramatically underperform the rest of the world it might also be in a climate of rising unemployment. Your job might be at risk. In such a scenario the exchange rate might be declining sharply. This in itself might result in inflation spiking and your costs of living getting worse.

Wouldn't it be better in such a scenario to have plenty of your investments being cushioned and not falling as much because they are priced in global currencies? I would think the answer is yes.

The downside of my point here though is when you own unhedged global equities and your own currency appreciates substantially. This waters down your returns. However in this environment you are probably more likely to have more stability in your finances. Probably more likely you are holding onto your job, most of your assets are rising, your income might be going up etc.

One of my key points on the topic of currencies though is the same point I made with asset allocations. Choose something you will stick to and rebalance consistently in the future.

Trading / Market Timing, does it make sense?

I am going to be boring here and side with most value investors in believing these strategies are generally not worth pursuing for a large majority.

One aspect of it that I am open minded about though is shorting the major equity indices such as the S&P 500 in certain circumstances. For me personally I would only entertain this thought when 1) valuation measures are indicating a very expensive market e.g. (CAPE above 20 at a minimum) and 2) it has moved below the 200 day moving average. The other criteria is in terms of position sizing, I am talking about a synthetic position size of no more than 10% of the portfolio.

In regard to the criteria mentioned in point 2 above, plenty of studies have illustrated that even with the potential increased transaction costs, you almost tilt the odds in your favour. Despite going against the long term bias of markets trending up, you come out with very similar returns. Obviously, the benefit is once again lower drawdowns, smoother returns over time. Also running broad short positions in market indices can pay off well if you view them as offsetting additional long positions. Provided of course that those additional long positions do better than the market you are shorting, which can be easier said than done sometimes!

One good book in terms of reading about various long term factors that make sense when investing in equities is "What works on Wall Street", by James P. O'Shaughnessy. The point I mentioned above is covered there along with many other interesting observations by the author.

Options, why not insure our portfolios like other things in life?

Should we buy put options on major equity indices to protect our portfolios? I would very rarely consider doing this. Regularly buying put options would be extremely costly over the long term. It would wipe out plenty of the eventual returns you expect when investing in the share market in the first place.

Yet if on occasions the cost of the premiums are being sold for dirt cheap levels I would not entirely rule out the idea. I remember in 2017 there were stories of amateurs selling put options for thin margins. Retail store workers starting up hedge funds with the strategy! Claims that it was the new normal and volatility was dead. It did not take too long for that to change! Below is a chart of the VIX, it even traded below 10 in late 2017.

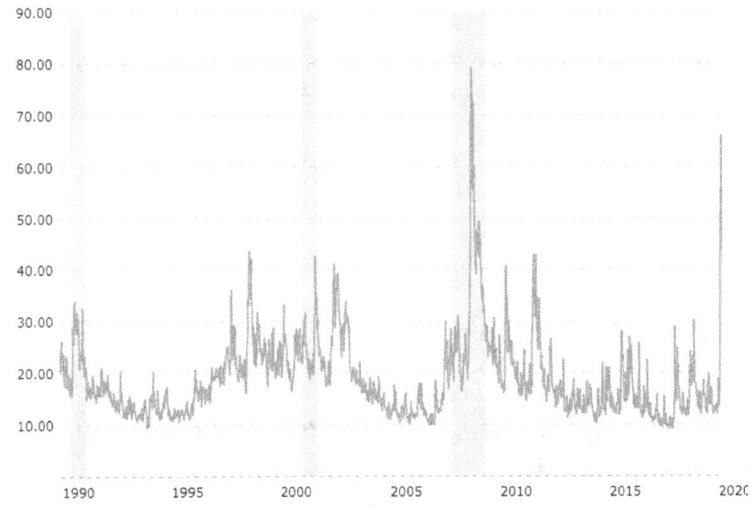

Source: https://www.macrotrends.net/2603/vix-volatility-index-historical-chart

You can see from above that when the VIX edges towards 10 it can be considered unusual levels of calmness in the markets. When buying put options during such times they don't cause as much of a drag on returns. They can then explode on the upside if you run into a bear market. You can see from above that there were opportunistic times to buy put options in the year or so before bear markets. I refer to bear markets in 1994, 2008 & 2020 in particular.

It is one of those things that most investors shouldn't bother with, it is a strategy for only those with a very active approach. Prior to those bear markets though one would assume investors might have achieved very outsized gains over the many years prior. They could then decide what small portions of such outsized returns they are prepared to give away if the put options become worthless as they often do. So to me in such circumstances, when the VIX is nearing the 10 level, I think owning put options in major equity indices is worth pondering.

DON'T COPY ME EXACTLY!

Once again I am going to repeat word for word what I wrote earlier. **Sticking with any strategy is difficult, so the good thing about the above points is the flexibility to choose a strategy that makes you feel comfortable. I would argue strategies with less drawdown risk are much easier to stick with over the long term!**

CHAPTER 6 - Why bother with ASX LICs / closed end funds?

I wrote a blog post quite a few years go titled "Where institutions avoid and retail investors find boring".

The statement summarises why good investment opportunities in these areas exist. Funds management institutions for a variety of reasons don't participate in these pockets of value as much, if at all. The benefits there are twofold. Firstly less competitive buying interest to push up prices of stocks that we are potentially interested in. Secondly it means we are trading in a less efficient marketplace because of fewer professionals scouting it. We are more likely to have "mum and dad" investors on the other side of the trade. An analogy if you like might be how serious poker players want to seek a table of weak players. The opposite would be to spend countless hours checking over the balance sheets of the four major banks thinking you can seek out the best performing one. You are competing with 100s of professional analysts spending their whole week trying to do the same!

LICs come about in the first place largely because they are issued at IPO to many smaller, time-poor investors. The stats show that buying LICs at IPO is generally a terrible strategy, so that says a lot about many investors who actively participate in this space. Most probably bought at IPO because they had a degree of trust in their broker who pushed the idea to them. Or they fell for the slick marketing campaign around the launch of the prospectus and lost sight of the fact they nearly always move to significant discounts.

There are a few reasons why professional money managers tend to ignore LICs. Although there is a wide selection of LICs of 100 plus on the ASX, many are quite small. It is not easy for fund managers to find many LICs with the desired size and liquidity, so that can put them off. Another reason I believe is the marketing aspect, and a bit of ego at play. They worry it is not such a great sales spin to say they have bought a LIC. Some clients might see that as outsourcing their job and effectively incurring an extra layer of fees. Whilst this might be true, there can still be such an extreme value proposition that they should not ignore the opportunities. Yet they may still do for this reason.

On the topic of investor egos my feeling is that many investors ignore closed end funds just because it comes across as relatively boring. For those that have the ability to invest in say sub $200 million LICs, it also means they could invest directly in micro caps themselves. That opens up a huge array of stocks where they can hunt for "ten baggers". You are unlikely to get such spectacular results in LICs, which means they can get neglected.

I am personally happy to rule out some spectacular results at the stock level though, if it also means less blow ups. It is far less likely typically for one particular LIC to fall as badly as a small stock might do. The more boring a style of trade is to me just implies less initial demand and there more likely to be better value there. From there we get more attractive opportunities on a risk / reward basis. That end result from a long term portfolio outcome point of view I find exciting rather than boring!

Heads you win, tails you also win?!

One of the key advantages to investing in LICs is capitalising on a large discount to NTA closing. There has been numerous occasions where I have purchased LICs with discounts at 20% and much bigger, and later realised the NTA value. If you can buy $1 of assets for 80 cents, this process can offer an additional 25% of returns aside from what the underlying investments produce.

The natural question to ask though is what about the cases where the discount stays wide, or even gets wider? That is where you have to back yourself to identify the right opportunities. Due to the LIC space being relatively inefficient with less sophisticated money around, this enables such opportunities regularly. Once again it comes back that analogy of finding a weaker poker table to play at. By focusing a lot on LICs, it is quite possible to be able to sift through the whole LIC universe and quickly sort out which ones are "value traps" and are not. Some LICs absolutely deserve to trade at discounts above 20% and have no decent prospects of closing the gap.

With the right ingredients in place, sometimes LICs are destined to close the gap to NTA whether they perform poorly or turn things around. Often (but not always) the LICs with larger discounts are suffering from some relative performance problems. If they manage to turn this around it is easy for the discount to move from 20% plus to at least in the 5-10% range very quickly. Even if it takes a few years that can still imply a "free kick" to overall returns of 5% per annum or so. This, combined with the actual good performance of the underlying fund holdings, can produce some strong results.

Yet should their underperformance continue then in many cases it produces the catalyst for the LIC to be wound up, and NTA returned to shareholders. We could be talking about an additional 25% of returns over a year or two of owning. That is a huge cushion to the risk you are taking. It might not even be because the fund has necessarily lost money during that time. A wind up might result because the fund has another year of underperforming a very strong market, or for other reasons.

Lower volatility from a top down and bottom up perspective

You can get a sense from the above type of situation that there is a natural tendency for the investment to experience lower drawdowns because of that wind up possibility. It is also likely to experience lower drawdowns because LICs will usually hold a very diversified set of underlying investments within them. When you combine some of these investments with the top down approach I mentioned in the previous chapter that limits drawdowns, it can make for very smooth returns.

Shareholder Activism and LICs

From the perspective of LICs, activists can be attracted to this space because attractive returns can be seen in isolation to "market risk".

Hypothetically consider a LIC at a 20% discount that holds a portfolio identical to the ASX200 benchmark. Therefore if nothing eventuates in terms of the discount changing, then the returns of the LIC will mirror the benchmark but may incur higher fees. The extra returns potentially available are from realising the gap between the 80 cents paid and the $1 of assets that sit there. These are returns that may be able to be achieved regardless of what the ASX200 does.

It could simply come down to convincing other shareholders to wind up the company. Perhaps selling down the portfolio and returning all funds to shareholders can be done with very little transaction costs. The "bet" in terms of the return from closing the discount to NTA can be about a different set of probabilities compared with working out the odds of whether equity markets are heading up or down. If hypothetically the LIC portfolio was the same as the ASX200 an activist investor could even hedge out all market risk by selling the relevant futures contract.

Of course it is important to weigh up such probabilities of closing the discount via activism correctly. The good thing in that respect is you do not typically read about a lot of other investors paying attention to this space. If we can uncover situations where activism has an 80% chance of closing a large discount within a year or so that sounds attractive to me. We don't have to predict whether markets are going up or down for such additional returns. These extra returns are not subject to the downside risk as much as market risk. For example when identifying the right opportunities, odds of the discount widening further can be quite low. Such additional returns of closing very large discounts like this are also often delivering as much as the overall returns we expect from equity markets.

Fortunately for smaller investors like us, thus far it doesn't appear to me to be a lot of sophisticated investors looking over these opportunities. There are some activists around though that might get to these situations first and crowd out some of the potential gains. However these are the guys we are relying on to do the heavy lifting for us. We need some other bigger investors to get to that crucial 5% stake at least and campaign for change at the LIC. The good thing is on plenty of occasions we are made aware of the presence of activists via ASX announcements and can sometimes even buy in at the same or even better price levels.

Efficiently accessing different asset class types

As good buying opportunities in LICs tended to dry up during the years between 2015-2018, it did result in a huge amount of IPOs created. Discounts had reduced substantially from the 2009-2012 period. This encourage a lot of new LIC products. Also after the AUD collapsed funds management companies later jumped on the bandwagon launching plenty of new global LICs. (after the horse had bolted in terms of the falling AUD tailwind of course!).

Anyway what it means is we have heaps more LICs than ever before. At the time of coming up with this book, I think we are talking about 120 or so. Prior to the GFC it was a bit less than half of that. The universe declined from a bit below 60 to closer to 40 post the GFC. Why did that occur? A big factor was large discounts to NTA and subsequent shareholder activism.

Another key reasons for this book is that I believe the LIC space is being set up well for some great opportunities over the next few years in terms of activism. We arguably have seen way too many LICs launched in recent years. That is ok because I hope readers of my blog were well warned to stay away from participating in them at IPO stage or shortly after. And to not pay premiums.

Many of the LICs launched around 2015 will soon be within the last few years of their investment management agreements (IMAs). This will make it far easier for activists to propose winding up LICs where it is appropriate. Plenty have not performed that well so this is well and truly on the cards.

Arguably due to financial advisors being incentivized to promote new LICs, we may eventually see some good opportunities again because of all the extra supply. Discounts of 25% plus with excellent chances of realising the NTA might pop up regularly.

With such a wide range of new LICs that got launched the last few years it can also help my investment style in terms of top down asset class diversification. In recent years we have seen a heap of new global LICs, and many LICs focusing on the small cap sector. The product range has even extended to more market neutral or long / short managers, those focusing on "real assets", and 2019 saw new LITs in the fixed income sector.

CHAPTER 7 - Why special situation investing and activism?

In the previous chapter I touched on the appeal of activist situations within the LIC sector. There were four key points to why such situations appealed to me.

1) There were potential extra returns aside from the "market returns" to be had.

2) Such opportunities are usually **neglected, as institutions are often too large to participate, and retail investors find them boring. Neglect can translate to the stocks being cheap**.

3) This type of investing often exhibits less downside risk compared with other approaches.

4) This all suits the audience to which I have in mind for this book. That is, an actively engaged private investor with a relatively small portfolio is in a good position to assess the probabilities correctly to seek such additional returns.

In terms of finding such events or special situation investing opportunities, one can follow the financial media closely for such situations. Another way to discover them might be setting up your own key word google alerts for the relevant terms. You might also follow certain similar styled investors and see these types of ideas from them as starting points for your own research.

How is special situation investing and activism linked?

Ideally investments need positive catalysts. Often the particular "event" needs management to take a certain strategic direction. As a shareholder we may have identified in our own mind that a specific strategy for the company is the way forward, but does management agree?

Although management always claim to be making decisions on behalf of shareholders, actions can speak louder than words. We have to be mindful that management may not necessarily hold much of the stock, that is have little "skin in the game". Even if they do hold a lot of stock, you would think then management should be aligned with the other shareholders right? Often the answer is yes, but not always. Although management may benefit from a stronger share price, they can sometimes benefit in other ways we cannot. They might be receiving excessive management fees, director fees, bonuses etc. Their remuneration over a long period of time well into the future could be more important for them compared with seeing that shareholder returns are strong.

The above scenario I painted where there is arguably a conflict of interest is where activism can be linked to some special situations

I look for. Situations where management want to entrench themselves in well paid employment for a long time (rather than worry about shareholder returns), can lead them to maintain a large company no matter what.

Maintaining a large company at all costs, or "empire building", can see them knock back some types of special situations that would otherwise be good for shareholder returns. Here are some examples where management could have a bias to in order to keep their jobs.

- Keeping an underperforming LIC listed at a persistently large discount to NTA.
- Refusing to engage in any takeover talks.
- Refusing to consider demerging a business from the company.
- Not paying out large franking credits on the balance sheet.
- Running a "lazy" balance sheet. Not making a capital return because a large company better justifies higher remuneration for them.

Deciding against the above and taking the opposite approach to such catalysts can often lead to a higher share price. Yet that may not interest management for reasons I have explained. We can therefore see how an activist present as a key shareholder can be greatly beneficial when searching for special situation investing opportunities.

Why shareholder activism is promising for the future, particularly on the ASX.

Now we can see that the presence of a shareholder activist can help unlock value in shares and mitigate the risks associated with management conflicts of interest. One reason in the back of my mind in searching for activism situations is there are some themes that I expect to be more prominent in the future. I shall briefly discuss such themes below.

Less research coverage on small caps – The sell side of the investment industry is finding it less feasible to produce research on small companies. This is resulting in cheaper valuations and bigger rewards for activists to unlock value. The activists themselves are usually prepared to conduct in-depth research, so have more of a competitive edge now in under researched areas.

Open mindedness in regard to board of directors – Certain trends in the make-up of the board of directors might be breaking down now. I am thinking in terms of the "old boy network" slowly becoming less relevant. This arguably used to encourage a lack of true independence amongst board members, and not making any tough decisions in case of upsetting others. The trend now is towards diversity, and a true independent board will be more receptive to activists ideas and whether they are in the interest of all shareholders.

Ethics – Ethical investing is rapidly growing area of interest amongst the investment community. The focus is more about the actions of the companies themselves and how they affect issues like the environment and other aspects that affect the community at large. The broad message though is for companies to be held more accountable for their actions. I expect this pressure to gain more traction in terms of pressure on company boards to be accountable in making sure they act in the interests of all shareholders. The spotlight should ramp up in examples where the board's decisions are more about feathering their own nest.

Social Media – Prior to the widespread use of social media it was far more difficult for smaller shareholders to let their opinions be known. Now an activist campaign could easily get momentum from one single relatively small shareholder presenting their case. If it makes sense enough there is no reason why the message cannot spread wide enough, leading to larger activists getting involved.

ASX relatively activism friendly – The ASX is considered by many experienced global investors to be an exchange with many rules around transparency and voting that are conducive to activism. The 5% threshold of ownership is very useful in terms of calling meetings. Also when an activist gets to this level they do have to declare their ownership in an ASX announcement, but they do not have to necessarily reveal any plans they have. There has also been increasing spotlight on management remuneration and the "three strikes rule" in Australia.

ASX an attractive area for activist funds to gravitate to – Numerous studies from www.activistinsight.com have noted that shareholder activism has been more of a trend in the US over the last decade or two. Investors such as Carl Icahn, Bill Ackman, Dan Loeb, Paul Singer, Nelson Peltz and others in that time have become even more well known. The activist strategies have been relatively less apparent thus far in Europe and even more so in Japan and other parts of Asia. Many expect that is due to change and Australia might also come under more attention.

Activist funds already in the media more with LICs – As discounts have widened in LICs since 2016 some activists have started making more noise in the media. Some of them you might already have been aware of for some time. For example we know Wilson Asset Management throughout their history makes a habit of buying into other LICs and make the necessary changes. Around 19/20 though I observed some newer players mention themselves they would be looking at LICs more. Some global players have already established substantial positions in some underperforming LICs. I thought it would be worthwhile to jot down here some interesting investors to consider following when they go substantial in a LIC at a large discount to NTA. Here are some that spring to mind. The Global Value Fund, VGI Partners, Armytage investments, David Kingston, City of London Investments, 1607 Capita Partners might be some others that may be circling LICs.

Why would I adopt this investment style, shouldn't I buy great companies at a reasonable price like Buffett?

Firstly, do not get me wrong, Warren Buffett if he is not the greatest investor of all time, he is certainly close to it!

So should not we adopt his style then? My views on this are perhaps different to what seems to be the consensus. <u>Due to his success, the money he oversees is so large now it is lacking any relevance to how a lot of us should be managing our money.</u>

Fund managers are also generally striving to oversee large pools of AUMs and receive the juicy fees on that. That explains why on so many funds management websites you will hear the messages that they want so that they can apply to huge sums of money.

If a share market tip sheet style service springs up they also gravitate to larger stocks. There is no point them providing fantastic tips if their large pool of subscribers can never buy the recommended stocks at the recommended prices due to lack of liquidity.

So there are many participants in the investment industry that are set up to make returns from enticing large pools of money from outside investors, rather than necessarily from good investment returns from their ideas. A bigger focus becomes on selling a story to get hands on other people's money, rather than going with the investment process that may achieve the best risk / adjusted returns. We end up with too many marketing / sales experts rather than good investors.

If everyone is trying to do the same thing does that investment style suddenly become rather average? I am not suggesting such methods are not the way to go for some investors, rather that it is becoming a very competitive way to try and outperform. If all investors are looking for the same things (large, well known quality companies?) then what are the odds we can find cheap companies in such areas?

The Buffett type style in recent decades makes more sense when you are managing billions of dollars. Especially hundreds of billions of dollars! The bigger you are the harder it is to move in and out of positions. Hence the bias to own higher quality companies as you can stick with these for longer. You might also have a bias to purchase quite large companies to begin with, as that might be the only realistic option. There is no point buying a great smaller investment if it is only worth 2 basis points of your fund! It is not worth the time and effort researching it.

The marketing aspect of the Buffett copycats

Since most fund managers are looking to grow their AUMs to as large as possible, they want their investment style to appeal to as many as possible. Intuitively the general public believe that investing like Buffett is the way to go. They all get comfort reading monthly / quarterly reports from fund managers if they speak of companies they own that are high quality and well known.

Speaking of a small previously distressed company that is winding up its assets does not appeal to the masses. Even if it may have fantastic risk /reward attributes. Large fund managers are often too big to invest in such special situations anyway

Does investing in larger quality companies work?

It does if you are especially good at it. Same with so many different investing styles. Yet if the trend in popularity is to go down this path as I have discussed, it will be harder to prosper in an area if it is more competitive.

If we do not have great skills within this area then many investors might be disappointed. From just a "factor" type investing approach, there is no evidence that on average buying large quality companies delivers superior returns. In fact, the small cap value tilt is usually cited as a clear factor tilt that has worked over the last century. Admittedly this has broken down somewhat in recent times, but that might represent an ideal time to drift to this tilt again now. What is defined as "value" often does not capture so many quality companies. As soon as fund managers see them as high quality (great to write about in their monthly reports to appeal to the masses), they often trade at higher earnings multiples or versus their book value.

Now I get that high returns from small cap value might be tied in with them being riskier in the sense of more volatile earnings streams. My point however, is that individual investors can often invest with a longer term timeframe to ride this out. We do not have to worry about external investors tapping us on the shoulder asking why some have underperformed over the last few years. Then potentially wanting to redeem money and forcing us to sell some relatively less liquid stocks. So why not take advantage of all this as a private investor?

In terms of quality I am still a big fan of trying to find a great company where there is no need to sell. The compounding benefits are huge not mention the benefits of deferring taxes. I just believe we are probably better searching in the smaller end of the market. The "Buffett copycats" are becoming so widespread in the last decade that they are crowding out opportunities in the larger areas that they fish around in.

How would Buffett invest if he managed a few million dollars or less?

I would like to again repeat this quote from Buffett *""If I was running $1 million today, or $10 million for that matter, I'd be fully invested. Anyone who says that size does not hurt investment performance is selling. The highest rates of return I've ever achieved were in the 1950s. I killed the Dow. You ought to see the numbers. But I was investing peanuts then. It's a huge structural advantage not to have a lot of money. I think I could make you 50% a year on $1 million. No, I know I could. I guarantee that."*

The above quote sounds promising if you are managing less than this amount of money, or even a bit more. Although I am not suggesting we all have the skills of Buffett and expect to achieve 50% each year!

We can infer that I do not think he expects to get such high returns right now. He has far more money to manage and large companies he owns could not compound like that. It is almost a mathematical impossibility because otherwise large well-known companies would take over the entire economy if they kept compounding like that.

Special situations as an investment style, Buffett and other successful investors

He mentions the 1950s where he received the best returns, so how did he invest back then? By the way it is worth thinking about. If we take from then and even throughout the 1960s, Berkshire was compounding at a more freakish almost 30% per annum! Without writing another book about that alone, we can pick out a few key differences.

He has even spoke on this topic at AGMs specifically. Rather than emphasise buying great businesses at reasonable prices and holding for a long time, his answers have been different. If hypothetically managing smaller sums of money he emphasized finding "off the map" companies. For example they might be at extraordinary low P/Es, or even discounts to cash. Classic Graham stocks like this are likely to be small in size, not the ones that high profiled fund managers can play around in or write about in their monthly reports.

So why then do so many smaller private investors try and emulate the Buffett of the 2010s, and not that of the 1950s /60s? After all, he has said himself if he was managing smaller amounts he would adopt the strategy like he did in the earlier years.

Another point to note is that although shareholder activism has gotten more attention in recent years, Buffett himself was known as more of a shareholder activist in the earlier days. This was more of a feature in the 1950s & 1960s. As I have pointed out this was a period of less money under management, but stronger returns for Berkshire. Such activist campaigns though often meant they had to exit the stock in a few years rather than hold for decades. Back then it was not so difficult to find replacement stocks to own in the portfolio. Now of course it is difficult because Berkshire is so large. This is not a problem for smaller private investors.

Who are some other famous investors that chalked up circa 30% returns on an annual basis when they were small enough to adopt more of a special situations strategy? Joel Greenblatt from the mid-80s until the mid-90s was one example. Seth Klarman was in that ballpark in his earlier days for his partnerships through most of the 1980s when he was managing smaller amounts.

The common theme though is that when a fund manager gets quite successful through special situation investing strategies they usually have to drift away in terms of style as their AUMs grow. This also discourages ambitious fund managers to adopt this style to begin with. Most fund managers like the idea that they have the potential to grow their business into several hundreds of millions in AUMs, or more likely billions.

That is good news for the private investor who likes to hunt around in special situations. There is a very good chance there will always be opportunities. The odds of great investors crowding out opportunities are not so high because they move onto different styles of investing.

Special situation investing instead of holding cash?

In an earlier chapter when I discussed my asset allocation targets I spoke of a cash or "cash equivalents" bucket. We know what cash is but what did I mean by "cash equivalents"?

Personally, I regard this as securities that I am highly confident will turn into cash over the next few months, usually sometime within the next 6 months or so.

If markets suddenly plunge then I usually do not expect to be able to use my cash equivalents to deploy into new buying opportunities that may immediately arise. However if markets stay depressed for many months, I might be able to slowly recycle money out of this cash equivalents bucket into such new buying opportunities. The idea is that the cash equivalents bucket can not only retain and increase its value during a bear market. It may also possess optionality value in being able to potentially deploy the cash later into depressed prices. Of course we know cash could do that, but the problem is the opportunity cost that cash can carry in a bull market. The aim of the cash equivalents bucket is it also can produce much better returns than cash. It can also go close to capturing a lot of the upside still in bull markets.

Some special situations that immediately come to mind in this area would include the following. Takeovers, wind ups, stocks cum very large capital returns or special dividends, a large tender into an off market buyback, a low risk relatively liquid market neutral fund.

These can be more attractive to seek out as the bull market enters its mature stages. Buffett used the term "workouts" when discussing this type of alternative to cash approach. Once again it is an example of his approach on the 1950s / 60s when his funds were not so large. The general idea is that the risk of these type of investments are less about what the general share markets might be doing. It is more about assessing the odds of a particular corporate action taking place. E.g. takeover approval, a liquidation achieving a certain amount, etc.

CHAPTERS 8 TO 40 ODD?, THE EBOOK PART TWO?

The rest of the eBook was going to go in depth in explaining various real special situation investing examples. It was to expand largely on about 32 types (plus a few more) of special situations briefly mentioned in the below blog link. It should be easy to locate this at the top of my blog.

https://valueinvestingforaliving.com/2016/10/21/where-institutions-avoid-and-retail-investors-find-boring/

As of April 2020 I have put this at least on hold for the moment for a few reasons.

- I am not that convinced it is very helpful to a reader to read more of an expansion of the above blog post. The reality is that to be successful using such strategies is a lot to do with getting your toes wet ***gradually*** and getting directly involved yourself.

- Trying to make various rules and checklists to most of the above categories might be over simplifying things. I might easily leave out some subjective traps an investor might fall into.

- When I got to April 2020 markets were moving around faster than I had imagined! When starting this eBook in January things were fairly boring. I expect 2020 could be busier for me in terms of trying to exploit the various special situations I emphasize here. Already at a minimum I can see I might be participating in many opportunistic share purchase plans (SPPs, just one example of special situations) which have become more interesting with the new $30k limit. I therefore wish to concentrate fully on my own investing for the remaining part of 2020.

- I expect I will get around to tackling the remaining chapters, and the above challenges I mentioned in doing that. I just don't think it will be in 2020. Hence I thought I may as well leave this up to download on Amazon in the meantime. If I don't do that then the chapters I have wrote to date may lack some context if I release them in a couple of years. A key idea to the book is that when I started writing in January 2020, a passive investment in an index fund on US equities didn't look that appealing. This may or may not change as time goes on, but I didn't want that message to get stale.

- It has been interesting working on this at a time of coronavirus lockdown and travel restrictions, I have had some extra time up my sleeve. I hope that and expect that to change soon though!

As mentioned one can subscribe to my blog at
www.valueinvestingforaliving.com

My twitter handle is @SteveGreeny73

Thanks for reading.

MID 2024 UPDATE TO INCLUDE BRIEF EXAMPLES OF SPECIAL SITUATIONS ON THE ASX FROM THE YEARS PRIOR TO 2020

It seems like I may never get around to a more in depth look at examples of special situation investing on the ASX from the past to include in this ebook.

What I have decided to do is simply insert the information from my blog here that I was going to use a basis to expand on for this area.

It might still be helpful to some, and one can perhaps do their own digging into some of the historical ASX stock codes I mention to learn more.

By the way it is fair to say at this stage in 2024 I would have to concede I am largely wrong with my thesis almost 5 years ago that passive investing in indices like the S&P500 looks challenging!

Having said that, on the plus side I will note that some of the performance I have documented in special situations investing on the ASX on the site strawman.com has done fine for me. It has been a portfolio that I can sleep better at night personally, compared to if I were to own the S&P500 or ASX200 in Australia.

This was how it was looking in late June 2024. Over 6 years is starting to get a reasonable timeframe to examine. Close to 18% per annum is pleasing for what I consider a lower risk approach.

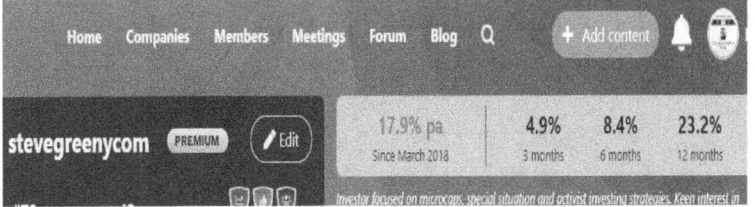

As I have tried to emphasize in this book, I value an approach that is likely to produce lower drawdowns than the overall market. This approach has been fairly consistent in that regard.

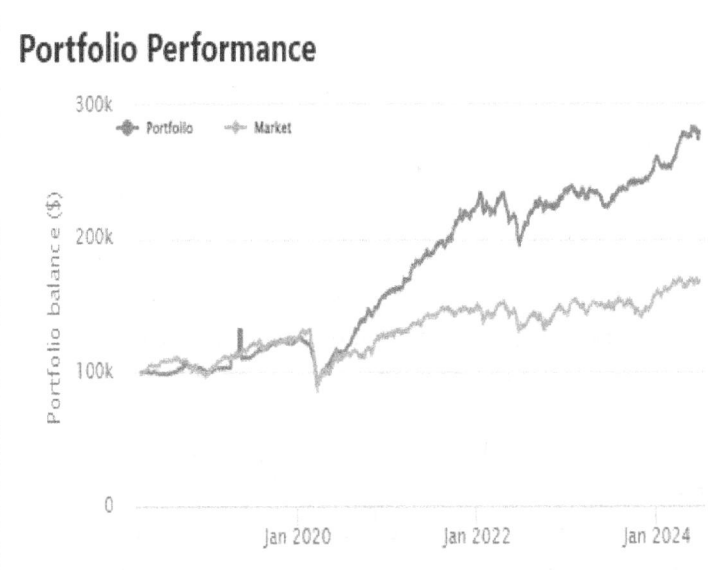

Below is the section I wanted to add from my blog that may better help readers get a feel for what sort of special situations I like to look for on the ASX.

WHERE INSTITUTIONS AVOID AND RETIAL INVESTORS FIND BORING

I meant to write this post when beginning the blog to assist in describing my investment style but it slipped my mind. It resurfaced in my thinking when I recently read a book Margin of Safety, by Seth Klarman. Some areas he cites in the book that are useful to look for opportunities are very similar to what I look for. It would also be great if readers can comment on any current "special situations" they see out there in the markets.

Aside from Seth Klarman's book, another one that is renowned for this topic is "You can be a Stock Market Genius" by Joel Greenblatt. The Klarman book wasn't in production for very long, and believe it or not currently is quoted on Amazon in a range of $US850 to $US1,500!

The title of this blog post sums up why certain situations in the market can often lead to better than average risk/return characteristics. There is a huge amount of dollars spent by major fund managers and brokers in analysing the bigger companies which can make that area arguably more efficiently priced. There are still opportunities I believe though because although the research can be quite in depth, the major players are often pressured by short term performance which can lead to misjudgements. Generally speaking, the more researched this space is results in fewer opportunities from mispricing. So areas where major institutions are not as prevalent should be where we should examine.

Some situations I find retail investors do not place enough value on investments that may be limited in terms of huge upside, yet have a high probability of very limited downside. They find it boring. I believe this partially stems from a lot of Australians viewing property as the way to slow and steady wealth building where you invest the vast majority of your assets, and the stock market as a place where you have far less invested and try and make a fast fortune. That helps explain the vast amount that is poured into speculative mining, biotech and technology plays over long time periods that don't on average produce good returns. An investment opportunity that shows a high probability of earning returns well greater than inflation (yet perhaps does not have the potential to quickly double in price) are often shunned by retail investors. For example, a company announces a wind up of a LIC and if the market stays flat perhaps there is a return of 7% awaiting in 6 months' time. Suddenly with the prospect of making large returns finished, many retail investors want to exit immediately and look for a new investment that offers greater upside potential.

I will try and briefly describe situations that meet the 2 criteria discussed above. i.e. where there is not as much institutional presence and where retail investors may sacrifice safer high yielding returns in favour of faster ways of growing their wealth.

Wind ups – discussed briefly above. I will add that a slow wind up can also help shareholder's tax position. For example, investors can receive a large portion of the market cap back in their pockets at a profit without paying CGT. Let's say you purchase a stock for $1, and management then plan to slowly wind up the company assets of $1.50 a share over a couple of years. Perhaps most of the assets are easy to liquidate meaning 90 cents is paid back to you in the first year. This just reduces your cost base to 10 cents rather than being a taxable event in the first year. I would also argue your typical equities manager doesn't spend so much time on these opportunities, they would prefer their quarterly market commentaries talk about strong growing and exciting companies instead. Some wind ups I have blogged about in the past include UPG, AIQ, GJT, & AJA.

LICs trading less than NTA – You will not see that many institutions will invest in another LIC. I don't think they enjoy the thinking that they are relying on another fund manager to do the job for them. Retail investors have a tendency to fall for the slick marketing and get involved often at peaks in the market and subscribe into floats of new LICs. They will pay $1 and sometimes the new LIC has costs of listing such that on day one they already only have 97 or 98 cents in the dollar to invest. "Free" options may also partially limit the upside. In nearly all cases they then begin to trade at discounts to NTA, in some cases in the order of 20 to 30%. Strangely retail investors then decide they are angry with the manager about the discount and it is time to sell, precisely when they should often consider buying!

REITS trading less than NTA – Similar comments to above. I would add the desire for most retail investors to have property exposure via their own physical residential real estate holdings also arguably can assist in pricing REITS more attractively.

LICs / REITS trading less than NTA and unusually listed on an overseas exchange – Taking the above two themes, I also keep a close eye on them when they have an unusual location of listing. Thinking of successful examples I have blogged about include VNL:LN, GJT, AJA, UOS. Among this bunch we have a Vietnam property fund listed on the LSE that was voted to be wound up. We have two Japanese REITS on the ASX that eventually got bought out. Then a property developer in Malaysia but which has a great track record of generating returns for Australian shareholders with their ASX listing. Nagacorp was not a REIT but unusual in being a Cambodian casino listed in HK.

Other unusual exchange listings, NSX? – Perhaps it can be fruitful to glance at the National Stock Exchange of Australia (NSX) and keep a brokerage account that can trade on this exchange. It handles smaller listings and likely not an investible proposition for institutional mandates. I acquired some shares in Asset Resolution Limited (ASS) that appear to be on the right path. It requires patience with virtually no volume at times but I got some shares mainly early 2018 at an average fill of 2.27. Company just a few months later since bought back lots of stock from very small holders willing to pay 2.88 to mop them up. I hang on to mine since I think management are keeping costs low (this is where the NSX can help it is cheaper) and are very competent. It has an asset backing of over $3 a share cash with some small hope or free optionality on potential proceeds from legal action. (so another special situation category this fits under is my later headline under "legal action pending").

Who knows whether the above will turn out well though, and I can't claim to have banked many profits from monitoring the NSX. Many of the situations in this post here I have noted for the purpose of future reference for my own behalf to remind me to keep searching certain areas of the markets. I have seen Tony Hansen at EGP Capital make some wise investments via the NSX which has made me more alert to the potential. Also have listened to Andrew Brown from East 72 holdings explain why the NSX can be an economical way to list a small investment company.

Hybrids – These often don't fit cleanly into institutional mandates so it can result in less institutional presence. I find the retail investors these are marketed to are not very sophisticated. Also the securities often contain a wide variety of features that they do not understand. This can make this area worthwhile to look for opportunities. In recent times hybrids from Crown Ltd and Elders in the secondary market have provided good opportunities for those that did the research. Unfortunately not me :(. SVWPA though is looking better for me.

Hybrids part 2 – In terms of not fitting cleanly into institutional mandates, it is even more apparent when we are dealing with credit rating downgrades. It is common for some mandates to be forced into selling a security because it is downgraded below a minimum rating criteria. The Multiplex security was a good example of this where some astute buyers took advantage of after the GFC. This area may make interesting hunting ground when Australia suffers its next recession.

Takeovers – Once a takeover is announced the share price will generally gain significantly on the day. Investors both institutional and retail are often overjoyed and want to quickly take profits and move onto another opportunity. They may have just made 30 or

40% on the day and now that stock is very unlikely to have another 30-40% upside left. This especially leads to retail investors moving on. They forget that perhaps in a friendly takeover there may only be another 5% upside but what if the funds can be received within 4 months and because it is friendly there are very little risks involved? Annually that may be a very attractive return. In a hostile situation perhaps another bidder may come along and some bidding tension result in the final bid another 20% higher? One must be wary of binary situations where one bidder may walk away and the share price could fall substantially. Institutions are often overly scared of reporting such a situation to clients so they will tend to sell too conservatively to completely eliminate such risk. If you are prepared to take on this risk, there may be the odd bad result but if you play this game long enough over time the average risk/return profile tends to stand up extremely well. I have had some hits and misses here in recent times with the likes of WCB, WTP, YBR & MUA.

Rights Issues (part 1) – Retail investors may often be strapped for cash to take up renounceable rights issues. Or they just do not want to increase their exposure too much in a company so they have a tendency to sell on market where they can the renounceable rights. If one likes the underlying investment this may provide an attractive way of entry. Institutions may pass up on the seemingly attractive arbitrage as they are probably focused on bigger decisions and getting involved would mean work for the corporate actions department.

Rights Issues (part2) – I am referring here to when a company makes a rights issue for good reasons. Perhaps for example an acquisition that is viewed by all as making sense then it may lead to a little short term indigestion of surplus stock. Investors both institutional and retail within a day find themselves having increased exposure to the company. Institutions may have tight sector or company restrictions and may need to sell back to keep the weight the same. Retail investors often do not manage their cash well or to begin with run far too high stock concentrations meaning they also don't want to increase their exposure. This can perhaps be an opportunity in the underlying stock. COG (formerly AIK) did this a couple of times but I eventually felt this stock was making too much of a habit of it.

Share Purchase Plans (SPPs) – Looking at LICs regularly I see a lot of them. If I sell a LIC that is at a sizeable premium to NTA I usually hang on to a tiny token parcel of shares. You may get offered a SPP that is "in the money" down the track. Kind of like a free option in the bottom drawer. Now some may say you can only get $15k worth but it could be a relatively risk free quick gain of 5-10% on some occasions. You also may be able to participate on a separate account such as another holding in a company etc. Given some overseas destinations where I travel tend to be cheap, gains can still go a long way so I am not too proud to overlook such opportunities! I have seen GVF do a SPP that was in the money at the due date and as I update this FGG may be heading that way.

Scrip mergers – Similar to the rights issues retail investors don't like complicated administrative things to deal with and tax issues to consider, even institutions are in the same boat. This can mean complicated scrip takeovers and mergers can provide attractive entries into certain stocks. As I update this in September 2018 the Wilson LICs may fit this category with retail punters not bothering with the complications. On the surface WDE looks a cheaper entry to WAM. CYA (possibly if they use up tax losses) could be a cheap entry into WLE.

When thinking about complicated things retail investors may not want to deal with the Paperlinx Trust / Spicers securities conversion comes to mind, given the booklet was 232 pages long! So long to read it almost put myself off, which was costly as I eyeballed it at 2.5 cents in May 2017 but was slack to get around to it. I felt initial pain finally stepping up and paying up to 3.2 cents in August 2017 but now touch wood that pain seems to be subsiding.

Delistings – A retail investor may fear the process with a delisting, and an institutional investor may not have the mandate to hold, or it could be too illiquid for them. For example, quite a few years ago I bought the stock AYT for about 3 cents. It provided loans for investors to buy into the eventual failed plantation schemes and was in wind up mode. MVT were trying to take it over at 3.5 cents and as a tactic their bid expired quickly and the company would delist. Many sold at around 3.5 cents because of fear of the process. I hung on and received payments over 13 cents the next 3 or 4 years from the share registry even though it was never listed. The loans were enforceable (after a high profile, complicated and drawn-out court case) and largely paid back to the company.

Another delisting example also from Mercantile occurred mid 2018. I bought a small parcel of AKF mid 2018 (likely from a seller late June wanting a tax loss) for 2.1 cents. I was able to sell into the company buyback in August for 6.1 cents. They had a delisting plan but clearly stated they would do a buyback first. Just a few months before they had already been happy mopping up unmarketable parcels at around that NTA value of 6.1 cents. It is handy to be playing with a smaller portfolio than the institutions sometimes.

Legal action pending – I could use the example just given above in this category (AYT), where the market almost forgets or at least misprices the probability of an outstanding legal case. APW was another example a few years back. I still hold and have written plenty about but the way I came into this a few years ago which is interesting. It was already well under NTA but the icing on the cake was a legal case that they were probably unlikely to win. If they did win however it would add about 25% to the NTA, over time it appeared the market had just given up on this because it was rarely discussed and considered on balance unlikely. So it was like effectively paying nothing for maybe a 40% chance they could add 25% to the NTA. The share price eventually climbed about 25% not too long after the case when in fact they did win. Maybe a future example can be with Asset Resolution Ltd on the NSX I mentioned?

Spinoffs – Both retail and institutional investors may receive shares in a spinoff company that is suddenly very small for their portfolios. They have a tendency to not want to have to think about these new shares and to make things easier just sell them.

They are less price conscious as sometimes the holdings are small for them, this may create opportunities. Statistically the evidence shows this is certainly the case both in Australia and the U.S. Quite often the company being subject to the spinoff was not given much focus to from the parent, and once these shackles are broken can then outperform. I am embarrassed to say I was a seller of S32 near the lows that could have been a great example here!

On the subject of embarrassments here is another one in an effort to keep this post a bit more balanced and not all about things that have worked. Whilst trying to make some money on RKN as they had a bid for their accounting business I observed that their spinoff of GetBusy could be the type I look for. Perhaps Reckon investors would easily discard it being a nuisance holding for them listed on the LSE. Well the sale for RKN fell through and I didn't get around to buying GetBusy! RKN which I owned plunged and GetBusy went up about 50% after I looked at it! Anyway it is still an example of a spinoff working.

Potential demergers – Rather than waiting for a spinoff opportunity it may be attractive to speculate beforehand. Recently we saw Crown Ltd rise substantially with plans to demerge. A couple of months ago I mentioned how Sandon Capital had some research about the increased value in TTS if they were to demerge. If you had of invested in Fosters before they demerged TWH that may have been attractive. Often pre demerger the companies have been underperformers and shunned by retail and institutional investors.

Taxation (part 1 franking availability) – Some companies have large capacity to pay franked dividends where they are currently not utilizing appropriately. Many institutional fund managers are set up such that these are not as valuable in a managed fund compared to say an individual receiving them in their directly managed SMSF. Retail investors probably may not even be aware the company has this capacity on their balance sheet. Therefore, they may represent undervalued situations in the market.

REF eventually paid out a huge special dividend to me, thankfully after the stock had previously been terrible for me. A dividend was declared of 5.5 cents which was pretty much where the stock price was only a couple of months earlier! TBR was quite successful in this regard. Management had some hidden value to some by holding their physical gold on the balance sheet at cost. Eventually a large part was sold for huge profits paving the way for a fully franked dividend worth half of the market cap.

Taxation (part 2 large losses to carry forward) – Some often poorly performed companies historically may have done so poorly much of the business has ceased. They could represent a small shell company with is little as under $10 mill in cash waiting for a new future direction. Sometimes they may well trade significantly less than the cash they have in the bank. If an acquirer can buy the company out and keep the direction of the company for the same purposes, there could be significant hidden value in the tax losses. For example, and oil and gas explorer/producer buying out another oil and gas explorer/producer. The same company purpose is needed to offset the losses against future gains to reduce tax. Also when companies are very small they can be attractive for "backdoor listings". If another company needs to raise funds then acquiring a listed shell company may be far easier and cheaper than doing your own ASX listing, so there may be hidden value in this also. It is not inconceivable a company with a market cap of $5 mill, trades at a market price of $3 mill whilst having prior tax losses on the balance sheet in the order of tens of millions. This may very much suit an acquirer! One needs to however treat these with caution. The risks are that the current management suck cash out of the company quickly and just want to keep their jobs with little concern for shareholders. You want to see an activist shareholder already present to extract the values, management to have some skin in the game or become the activist yourself. NGE became a LIC that I blogged about that soon began to highlight its huge tax losses to the market in regular NTA updates. Unfortunately I missed out on good gains in this stock as wasn't holding when they had most of their big run!

Tax loss selling – I wrote about this here…

https://stevegreeny.com/2016/06/02/tax-loss-selling/

Companies with large single holdings – Sometimes a company, often an LIC may run a concentrated position in another company and the market is slow to react if that holding surges in price. Some examples in recent years that spring to mind are HHV had 20% of funds in Sirtex, MVT had 40% funds in INA, HHY had 30% funds in CSE, CSE have nearly all their funds in SYR etc. As discussed above institutions are usually not present in LICs, and often the retail investors trading them do not watch the underlying investments of the LIC very closely. This year on the blog I have timed entries into HHV, GVF, HHY, TOP, SNC and particularly NCC recently quite well I believe due to other investors not paying close enough attention to the underlying holdings of the LIC.

Director or "insider" buying – I feel you have to be very selective here. The amounts should be significant for the director involved in terms of personal wealth, and ideally they have a decent track record investing themselves. Have seen plenty of examples of some director buying at peaks in the market so it is just a tool to use with discretion.

Company buybacks – Like director buying just mentioned you need to be selective here also as there are plenty of examples on average that companies buy back their shares at precisely the wrong time. I think it is more of a signal to watch when used in LICs or REITS trading at a discount to NTA. If you can sense the balance sheet allows and the company has hinted a buyback may be imminent then a purchase in anticipation of the buyback may prove a solid entry point.

Company inclusions / exclusions in major stock indices benchmarks – In recent years' active managers around the world are having on average a terrible time with performance, so I expect the growth in ETFs and index investing to continue to be strong. This is likely to present more opportunities in taking positions that can capitalize on index funds being forced buyers or sellers in certain companies being included or excluded from benchmarks.

Small companies in general – The smaller the company is obviously the larger institutional fund managers cannot invest in it to obtain a stake that is meaningful in terms of their own portfolio. The smaller the company it is the more likely you are placing your investment skills against participants in the market that are less sophisticated.

Illiquid small caps – this can be an area suitable for me given my modest funds to manage. Convention would say this is a major negative. This view, and the fact that many fund managers can not get set in a position, can see some good investments get bypassed by many knowledgeable investors. Ideally they are situations where I am not reliant on selling on market any time soon. That could mean the business is sound enough to hold for many years. Maybe it pays the return via regular dividends, or regularly can buy back shares, or perhaps it involves a slow wind up of assets. An impatient investor who needs out may provide a bargain due to selling at very cheap prices because of the illiquidity.

Lost mandates and forced selling – This can impact smaller companies more severely. Shareholders owning greater than 5% in a company will have to disclose when they are reducing this my more than 1%. Occasionally there may be situations where you discover this selling matches the news about the manager having lost an investment mandate. The client behind the mandate may not give the manager much discretion and this could be an opportunity, the selling may be done with little regard to the valuation at the time.

LIC options – I added this recently because over the last few years there has been a surge in new LICs come to the market with "free" options. I haven't found many buying opportunities yet but suspect it may be a good hunting ground. In the example of spinoffs, the average punter often sees the spinoff company as a tiny new share holding of nuisance value and can end up selling without any thoughts about the underlying value of the security. I can see in the future many participants in LIC floats in recent years will firstly quit in frustration at a discount to NTA. They then also may sell the options into thin markets with no research at all about their value. Another scenario is they simply are short of cash to exercise the options in the future anyway. Here they also may sell the options on market, and because the value of the trade is likely to be small they may not bother with much research as to their underlying value.

LIC catalysts options expiry and dividends – The share price of LICs with large overhang of options can often find it difficult to perform. I notice as this overhang is dealt with it can lead to quite a positive re-rating of the LIC. Another factor that can kickstart a LIC share price that is suffering is the announcement of an inaugural dividend or a big increase in dividend. The good thing about this is it is often telegraphed to investors if you bother to read the annual and half yearly reports (which many LIC investors don't). If you follow the profit reserves, franking, and how the portfolio is going including sales they have made in the period, you can get a good insight. I was buying SNC in the second half of 2016 partially on this basis. It appeared the announcement of a large franked dividend in early 2017 was the turning point and for awhile led to them trading at a premium of nearly 10% to NTA. Quite dramatic when there was a discount of about 15% at times in the previous year, and this large dividend was always quite predictable if you listened to what management were saying.

Hidden value within accounting policies reading the notes sections of the accounts – Stocks I have held such as TBR, UOS & SRS have had assets recorded at levels lower than their realistic worth. This can keep them under the radar to some extent on certain quant filters. In the case of UOS & SRS some properties being valued at cost and TBR had huge amounts of gold likewise at cost.

Companies in ugly industries but not reflective of the entire business – An example that springs to mind would be investors turning up their nose at Fairfax in recent years without doing their numbers on Domain that was later a spinoff. SRS was an ugly company, commercial print would cause many to not take a second look. But in 2017 a heap of net cash, room to slash costs made it less ugly. Likewise other facets such as signage & display, packaging and digital media solutions weren't as ugly. One of my positions in JYC hasn't done much for me. I wonder if the perception of it being old style bricks and mortar retail turns off investors. It shall be interesting how much profits come from the recently acquired Lloyds online auctions in the longer term.

Commodity Royalty Assets – I am more flagging this here for my own reference rather than claiming I have invested in this space much in the past. I found the Sandon presentation on Iluka regarding a potential spinoff of their Iron Ore royalty asset very interesting. I did profit well on ILU but I don't think as a result from this event or its potential. Yet looking at Sandon's point that these assets can be valued more fairly on the US exchange, I wonder whether there is more hidden value in this area on the ASX?

Failed IPOs – Some IPOs that have missed earnings forecasts that were laid out in the prospectus within their first couple of years can be an interesting place to look. It reminds me a little of the LIC cycle, i.e., they get marketed so heavily at the float, so they can be vulnerable a year or two in. They arguably get sold to "weak hands" and show a tendency to over promise at the prospectus stage. Weak hands then sometimes overreact a year or two in. In some cases, the actual company is not doing all that bad, it is just a case of overly high expectations and being sold to impatient investors in the first place. SSG is a stock that I own that might in some ways reflect this cycle.

Merry Christmas trading! – This might be considered a weird one. Look I know most of us prefer to relax in that slow period in the markets, especially say from towards December 20th through to the first week of January in Australia. Yet liquidity is very light so price swings can be irrational in micro caps. If you think you have good knowledge of the microcaps on your watchlist it can be fruitful to not fully switch of your screens over Christmas. Perhaps you can receive a gift being on the opposite end of someone over panicking to some news. Or maybe it is a stock that doesn't rise as much as it should on good news. It is not too dissimilar from how I mentioned that end of year tax loss selling in June can bring up opportunities.

Ethical investing?? – I don't want to give out examples here as these days it is very easy to offend! I will just say that this area is growing rapidly. Now in most cases you might totally agree with the increasing number of stocks that are put on the banned list by fund managers. Not owning it yourself is a fair enough stance to take so good on you. However if you don't find a stock unethical but a lot of the market does, my guess is it trades at much cheaper multiples these days. This could be an opportunity if you see potential returns via dividends / capital returns / buybacks. The reason I say that is because it might be tough to sell to other investors. But if you treat it like a business owner where management is acting fairly and letting you share in the future income stream that may not matter.

For an investor like me who seeks to limit drawdowns on the portfolio, yet still achieve returns greater than inflation to help make a living, these areas can be rewarding to examine. These are areas I have written down in the past for myself to look for. They are also very similar to one of the chapters I read in Seth Klarman's book. Though here I have just written as briefly as I can and more directly linked to my own experiences on the ASX.

www.ingramcontent.com/pod-product-compliance
Lightning Source LLC
Chambersburg PA
CBHW070417220526
45466CB00004B/1437